LANGUAGE
AND LINGUISTICS

LANGUAGE
AND LINGUISTICS

AN INTRODUCTION
TO THE STUDY OF LANGUAGE

J. F. WALLWORK

SENIOR LECTURER
FURZEDOWN COLLEGE, LONDON
FORMERLY LECTURER IN ENGLISH
UNIVERSITY COLLEGE, NAIROBI

HEINEMANN EDUCATIONAL BOOKS
LONDON

Heinemann Educational Books Ltd
LONDON EDINBURGH NEW DELHI
MELBOURNE AUCKLAND TORONTO
IBADAN NAIROBI JOHANNESBURG
HONG KONG SINGAPORE

ISBN 0 435 28930 6 (hardback)
ISBN 0 435 28931 4 (paperback)

Published by
Heinemann Educational Books Ltd
48 Charles Street, London W1X 8AH

Made and Printed in Great Britain by
Cox & Wyman Ltd
London, Reading and Fakenham

Contents

Introduction

There is nothing new about the study of language; men have been interested in, and concerned about language for thousands of years. Over the centuries scholars have made careful and detailed observations about, or analyses of, their own or other languages, and although I have no means of confirming the judgement, it is sometimes said that the best grammar yet written is that of Pānini, who in about 300 B.C. produced a grammar of Sanskrit which for accuracy and elegance has yet to be surpassed.

But like many studies, the study of language has had its vicissitudes and its changes of fashion, and again like many other studies, the conditions created by twentieth-century thought have caused men to look at familiar studies in unfamiliar ways. The voluminous and marvellously detailed observations of the English language made by the great grammarians such as Jespersen, Kruisinga and Poutsma may have seemed to represent almost the ultimate in careful and accurate analysis of a language. But then something apparently new appeared in academic discussions, and, in due course, in prospectuses and syllabuses—the study of 'linguistics'. There was, and is, considerable confusion, doubt and ambiguity about just what 'linguistics' is. To some it seems equated with 'grammar', to others with 'philology', to others it appears to be some kind of bastard science, or pseudo-mathematics, and to yet others it suggests something vaguely psychological. There are grains of truth in all these assumptions, for linguistics is essentially a meeting point for many disciplines, but in itself, it is just that plain, old-fashioned thing, the study of language.

But in the twentieth century there are new, and one likes to think, better, ways of studying language than those followed in previous centuries, or perhaps it would be better to say, ways have been found of extending and deepening earlier insights. Much new and interesting thinking and research is in progress, but few modern linguists would claim today that they are anywhere but at the beginning of a full understanding of the many complexities of linguistic study. To many it may seem premature for such tentative and incomplete studies to figure on school and college syllabuses, but increasingly 'linguistics' appears as a subject for study in all sorts of courses. Provided that linguistic study is treated as a series of interesting, and often useful and enlightening, hypotheses, and not as a collection of indisputable facts, there would, however, seem to be nothing but good in trying to help people understand more clearly that instrument by which we almost all conduct our lives. In particular it seems necessary that anyone with any professional concern for language, and this means, especially, the teachers, should have some insight into how linguists are thinking.

Unfortunately, many of the more interesting findings are available only in rather difficult, and sometimes inaccessible publications, and it is not easy to find something to read which will be simple and direct and yet open up the way to more detailed study if required. This book is an attempt to provide this starting point. Because it had to be reasonably simple, it is open to the charge of over-simplification; because it had to be selective it will surely omit some things which any one reader would want in. More specifically, it cannot, except fleetingly, refer to the vast amount of interesting research in progress in the U.S.A. and elsewhere overseas. Obviously any such book is personal, and contains what the writer thinks important. But if it is personal it cannot be, except marginally, original, and could not have been written without the findings of all those authors listed in the bibliography and undoubtedly others whose original thinking has passed into common linguistic currency. Nor could it have been written without the stimulus of attending lectures and seminars at University College, London, 1965–66, and the encouragement and help of family and colleagues, both earlier than this in East Africa, and later, in London.

London
September 1968

I

What is Language?

At least one book has been entitled 'What is Language?'
'What is water?' asks a ten-year-old child. He is, rightly, not
satisfied that it is 'what you drink'; nor is 'what we speak' an
adequate answer to the first question. The child is no more
conscious of learning to speak than he is of the great cycles of
nature that eventually lead to the kitchen tap. He usually takes
both for granted, language no doubt more than water. The
complex explanations of what water is, its chemical constituents, how it arrives via the rain, lakes, rivers and waterpipes
to the tap are ultimately much easier than the explaining of
language; the fact of death without water is rapidly comprehensible to the child; the probably equally disastrous if less
immediate consequences of life without language in a modern
civilisation are less apparent even to the more sophisticated.
But if 'What is Language?' is for the moment, difficult to
answer, it is perhaps possible to begin by looking at the various
uses people make of language.

The currently fashionable way of describing any use of
language is to say that is for 'communication'. As the Scottish
correspondent of the *Times Educational Supplement* said recently,
'Reading, writing and spelling are unmentionables, but the arts
of communication (being integrated), may be discussed with
propriety.' 'Communication', however, is too vague to be of
much use. Dogs communicate when they bark or wag their
tails, so do chimpanzees when they use sound, or facial and
bodily gesture; wolves in a pack, or bees in a hive, work with
obvious co-ordination which must be derived from some form
of communication; as Sapir pointed out, even the clouds in the
sky can be said to communicate the imminence of rain; computers can certainly answer back. But the languages all these
use for communication are, without exception, of a very

I

restricted kind, in spite of the apparent complexity of the computer, and are evidently different in ways other than degree of complexity from human language, so 'communication' must be more narrowly defined, and yet cover more, than these other restricted languages if it is to be applied to human language. Let us examine some ways of using human language.

Jones is exercising his dog in the park and meets Smith with his dog. Jones says cheerfully, ' 'Morning, Peter. How's things?' Smith grunts and says something that sounds like 'So-so'. Jones's dog growls and then bares his teeth. Smith's dog bristles and raises his tail. Jones's use of language has probably communicated (*a*) a desire to be friendly, and (*b*) his optimistic view of life at that moment. Smith's grunt, and words, communicate (*a*) his lack of interest in Jones's society, and (*b*) his less optimistic view of life. The dogs have communicated a warning and a defensive reaction. Had Jones said, 'Nice day today, isn't it?' he would have communicated pretty well the same thing as he did by 'How's things?' The exact words he uses are largely irrelevant to the situation, and a choice of any one of a fairly restricted set of phrases would have done equally well. Not so long ago much more formal emphasis was placed on teaching this sort of human communication; children stood up and said 'Good morning, Miss Smith,' as she entered the room; they were taught that the 'correct' response to 'How do you do?' was 'How do you do?'; and the person who interpreted the language literally and responded in the logical rather than the approved fashion, perhaps with 'Pretty lousy, thank you' immediately became a social outcast, not so much because of the lice, but because of the language. Loosening of convention in social life has meant that in many circles now the logical rather than the formal response is appropriate, but quite often in public life we still accept a response which is irrelevant to the actual language of the stimulus, or we use language with no apparent relevance to the actualities of the situation. To quote only two examples: in the Christian marriage service the Minister's demand 'Who giveth this Woman to be married to this Man?' is a rhetorical, formal demand bearing little relationship to legal or factual, or even spiritual life, but is nevertheless to many people a valuable and revered use of language. A later part of the same ceremony where the man says '... with all my worldly goods I thee endow ...' bears a meaning legally rather different and factually often very different from the literal meaning most users of the phrase would attribute to it. Parliamentary language may appear nonsensical, as when one member of Parliament who wishes to be offensive to another still feels constrained to say 'The Honourable Gentleman is a damned liar'.

In its private form this 'phatic' communion, as Malinowski called this part of speech behaviour which is mainly polite talk, greetings and rather meaningless exchanges of words, is socially necessary, but it is perhaps not so far removed from the communication of animals expressed in sounds such as barking, grunting, trumpeting, and so on, and in gestures such as baring the teeth, pawing the ground or wagging a tail. Phatic communion and animal language both serve to establish, consolidate and confirm social relationships. Human usage even here probably offers a wider range of differentiation than animal usage, reflecting the greater complexity of social ordering. Chimpanzee society, however, is thought to have fairly complex recognition signals, though unlikely perhaps to range the gamut of, for instance, 'Hullo!' (with varying intonations), 'Hiya!', ' 'Morning!', 'Wotcher!' (if this is really ever heard off-stage) 'Good morning, sir!' and the varying grunts which are all possible human greetings even in one human language.

But to return to Mr. Smith. If, later in his walk, he meets another, unknown man with a dog, and if this man bows and says 'Guten Tag, mein Herr', Smith is likely, apart from his surprise, to feel a little shocked and insecure. Who the devil was it—to speak to him in a language which, whatever it was, was certainly not English? And how much more the unease might have been if the man had looked Asiatic, or African, and the language had been obviously non-European. The stranger who says 'Good morning' is maybe eccentric, or even just extrovert; the stranger who says 'Guten Tag' deserves suspicion, at least in England. The use of a common language assures at least a degree of social cohesion; to speak the same language is, for most people, to give a sense of security, and of belonging. Smith abroad accepts 'Guten Tag, mein Herr', but unless he is of the small number of either English cosmopolitans or Anglophobes, tends to find much relief in an unexpected English 'Good morning' in his hotel dining-room.

Even within 'English', the speaking of a common form of English often strengthens personal and social bonds. Two businessmen both using Yorkshire dialect may well get on better than two, one of whom uses Yorkshire and the other Irish dialect forms. The particularly English tendency to 'place' a person, to adopt a particular attitude to him, based on the form of the language he uses, will be discussed later.

Private 'phatic' communion then, serves primarily to establish our social relationships with each other. There is a similar, more public, use of language which results from an attempt to control our environment by the use of words. The incantations of a primitive tribe to induce rain, the prayers to the Christian God for help in suffering, the ritual of a funeral ceremony which includes phrases such as 'earth to earth, ashes to ashes, dust to dust,' together with the philosophical reflection 'Man that is born of a woman hath but a short time to live, and is full of misery', the strictly defined utterances and responses that have to be made on state and legal occasions, all these in their different ways illustrate uses of language whereby we seek to soften the desolation of life, or to assure future wellbeing, either in life or death. Whereas the personal, phatic, communion establishes a social relationship between individual people or groups of people, the 'ceremonial' communion may seek to establish a relationship between man and god, or between man and some abstract and formal ideal. When such ritual and ceremonial use of language is very long established, it is possible that the original meaning of the actual words used is lost, and for the participants in the ceremony the words cease to have much 'meaning' in the literal sense, and as with the examples we saw earlier, the 'meaning' of the language will then derive not from the words, but from the fact of saying them in a particular context, at a particular time, without respect to what the participants might understand by a literal meaning of the words.

Hence perhaps derived the reason for the continued use, until relatively recent times, of Latin in much of Roman Catholic church services; the fact that hardly anyone who used it understood it perhaps didn't matter, for communication was established without reference to literal meaning. And possibly those who opposed the change of Latin to the vernacular, feared that to change the language too abruptly would in fact disrupt rather than enable, communication.

It is not, of course, true that in all ceremonial or ritual uses of language, choice of words is of such relatively minor importance; it is possibly only true indeed in the case of ceremonies where the participants do not feel very deeply about what they are doing, or are professing to be doing. Where personal human feeling is deeply involved, then the choice and use of words becomes of much more vital import, and in the past, wars were even waged over the exact interpretation of what a Church service might or might not say. Sometimes words have the power of action themselves. If during the baptism ceremony the child acquires the name 'Josiah Bloggs', this naming does something which has a pronounced and observable effect not only then, but for years afterwards. It is, moreover, an effect which might have been quite different if the clergyman had referred, not to 'Josiah Bloggs' but to 'William Henry' or 'John George'. In a Muslim country, the mere saying of 'I divorce you', in certain specified circumstances, itself constitutes an act, as in this country the words of a written will are themselves actions: 'I give and bequeath . . .' and the exact words used may have great and direct legal, social and emotional consequences. Only too familiar, again, is the dilemma good men have found themselves in when they have had to pronounce judgements or verdicts contrary to their own inclinations or beliefs, but dictated to them by the exact language of a law which they are bound to operate. The words of such laws can themselves constitute actions which cannot easily be escaped. Philosophers, and following them at a respectful and so far rather wary distance, linguists, have indeed begun to look at the distinction between such different uses of language as those where the act of speaking or writing has a certain force beyond

5

that of merely 'having a meaning', and those where there is no such force. In the first category might come such uses of language as exercising judgements, asserting an influence, making declarations of intention, or pronouncing verdicts of different kinds.

Apart from such relatively abstract classifications, however, it is obvious that in everyday life, there are many occasions when exactly what we say matters enormously, and has marked effects on the conduct of our lives. 'Eight pounds of potatoes, please,' fills our vegetable rack comfortably; 'Eighty pounds of potatoes, please,' would be a considerable embarrassment. A little 'y' sound makes the difference between good order and chaos in the kitchen. In using language to give orders, to control other people and things, a precise and logical use is necessary. No doubt there are some orders we can give without language at all—a look, a gesture, may sometimes be clear enough, but we will have some difficulty in getting our eight pounds of potatoes without language. The dog that jumps up, whines and barks alternately in his desire to be taken for a walk, has to repeat his gestures at considerable length to achieve the effect that Smith's wife achieves much more economically, and probably more effectively, by saying to her husband, 'Let's go for a walk' in a fairly firm tone of voice. Whereas phatic and ceremonial language may be meant to control the environment in a non-logical, incantatory way, our precise orders are meant to control it deliberately and consistently.

To some extent we control our present in the light of our past. A primitive people preserves its history, laws and traditions by oral accounts handed down from generation to generation. A more sophisticated society deposits its records in printed, written, taped or filmed form in acres of archives and libraries. Both are selective, the former perforce more than the latter. A sophisticated society will enshrine and petrify in written language what it considers worthy of record, a primitive society will keep alive, embellish and perhaps distort through the ages the source of its present state of being. No language, no history. Technology and science may control the environment, but they too rest upon language and the passing of information and commands, whether the language takes the form of complex mathematical symbols, or abbreviated jargon, or highly complex sentences.

Many people, if asked what they think language is used for, will give as their first answer, its use in the passing on of facts and information. The other uses of language tend to appear less significant, largely because modern society is so fact-orientated, and in such a society language is of course very important. Indeed, such use is virtually indispensable to comfortable living. Someone asks, 'What's the time?' and we answer 'It's nearly two o'clock', or someone yells down the stairs, 'Where are my clean socks?' and we answer 'In the top drawer'. Or we are confronted with a tin of syrup, firmly closed until we read 'To open this can, insert a penny under the rim of the lid'. Such factual uses of language are essential to the smooth running of daily life. But the mass of verbiage from all over the world in every issue of the day's papers, the streams of fact and alleged fact poured out over the air in radio and television programmes lead, guide, cajole, persuade, entreat or disgust us as well as inform us, according to the whims and intentions of thousands of unknown, and usually faceless, men and women. We may tend to regard these uses of language (news reporting, factual articles, etc.) as the 'passing on of information', but it can be argued that while conveying fact, they also tend to bring the status of 'fact' into question. By the inevitable selection of fact, the fact itself becomes both less and more than a fact. Again, the often emotive use of language used to report a 'fact' adds an extra quality only too often not distinguished from the fact itself. The emotive use of language, particularly in so far as it influences people in matters of what they believe to be fact, is something to be considered fairly fully later in the book.

Is there anything in common between a hearty 'Damnation!' and the strains of 'Marriage of Figaro' issuing from the bathroom? The 'Damnation!' might have been something less socially acceptable, the 'Marriage of Figaro' might have been 'John Brown's Body . . .' and it would not have been of significance except in so far as the tastes and interests of the persons were possibly revealed. As with 'phatic' communion, there is a

7

relatively restricted range of appropriate swear words in any one language, but again as with phatic communion, selection from the range is largely immaterial, for the use of language in these cases is largely one of self-expression, independent of the actual sense or content of the words. With the singer, the words may exist only in tum-ti-tum fashion, or even if in more recognisable form, are likely to be irrelevant to the purposes to which the vocal organs are being put. In both cases some form of language is being utilised simply as a means of 'getting something off one's chest'—good or bad. This is self-expression in a primitive and unoriginal way, sometimes, as in the case of singing in the bath, coupled with sheer pleasure in the sound itself. A baby may babble, often with the more unconsciously determined aim of exercising the muscles required for speech, but perhaps also sometimes with sheer pleasure in the sound itself?

To the relief and pleasure of such primitive linguistic self-expression is ultimately related the self-expression which we call literature, especially poetry, though not all literature, or even all poetry can be included here. Such expressive literature is a deliberate attempt to give linguistic shape to humanity; to mould experience, emotional and social experience, into the shapes laid down by the linguistic community and, where necessary, to expand and enlarge the shapes in order to fit new or newly perceived experience. 'Damn' is immediately comprehensible because it is a simple linguistic expression of a pretty simple human reaction.

> *Glory be to God for dappled things—*
> *For skies of couple-colour as a brinded cow;*
> *For rose-moles all in stipple upon trout that swim;*
> *Fresh-firecoal chestnut-falls; finches' wings;*
> *Landscape plotted and pieced—fold, fallow and plough;*
> *And all trades, their gear and tackle and trim.*[1]

may be less immediately comprehensible, because the human reaction is now no longer simple and therefore not easily given conventional linguistic expression. It is probable that truly obscure literature remains obscure not because of the difficulties

1. Gerard Manley Hopkins, *Pied Beauty*.

of the language, but because what it attempts to convey is not a genuine experience or reaction but a forced or untrue one. The 'obscure' literature, which is a genuine expression of humanity, will eventually be understood even if the language has temporarily outstripped the conventional provisions and is not immediately accessible to its contemporaries. Language which fulfils a genuine need or expresses a genuine human reaction may be difficult to understand because of its linguistic novelty or because of the novelty of the concept or reaction behind it, or both, but will ultimately find an audience, if only a limited one, to whom it is not obscure.

I have mentioned, at least by implication here, the relationship between language and feeling or emotion, and have again by implication rather than by direct statement suggested that, so to speak, the emotion came first and the language had to follow after, at least for the poet, though the process may be reversed for the reader. It is however not quite clear whether this is the right order of things, and when the relationship between language and thought is considered it is even less clear what, if any, is the 'right order'. Does language follow thought? Can thought exist independent of language? There is no simple answer to these questions and there is not likely to be any. Psychologists have much work left to do on the thinking processes, and even they are unlikely to produce any simple or single answer, although work on the relationship between language and concept formation has been explored in some depth. There are many kinds of thinking—some of which seem inextricably tied up with language, others of which seem to be less dependent on it. It seems, for instance, probable that language plays a minimal part in the 'thinking' required of us by the roadside posters exhorting us to 'Think before you overtake', or with what we mean when we speak of a tennis player's 'thoughtful game'. That there is a close relationship between thought and language is obvious; the commonly heard 'I know what I mean, but I don't know how to explain . . .' suggests the possibility that in at least some cases thought can be, and often is, independent of ordered language. Research now in progress suggests strong links between a person's linguistic

9

resources and his flexibility towards new ideas, or his ability to progress educationally. For the moment it may perhaps be simply left by saying that for most people, it is difficult to 'think' in the sense of to deliberate, or reflect, beyond the bounds set by their linguistic competence, and that thinking beyond these bounds requires a deliberate effort of originality or an original insight open to few. Should there be an original act of thinking, or an original insight, it remains to find the language to fit it, and again, only a few may be able, in the first instance, to understand the language. For most people language and thought are mutually interdependent; we cannot think, except with confusion and difficulty, what our linguistic competence does not permit; we cannot utter what we cannot think.

To some extent, then, we are controlled in our thoughts and actions by the language we know. No two languages are identical, and it has been suggested, therefore, that people with different mother tongues will have different responses to things, based on their different languages. Just how different two languages may be is illustrated by the common difficulty of translation from one tongue to another. Where translation is of something which can be related to a visible stimulus, there is a fair chance of verifying that both versions relate to the same occurrence, though even here there may be initial room for doubt. Alone in a foreign country, an English speaker sees a snake glide by and a native says 'Nyoka!'. Should he assume the correct translation is 'Snake!' or 'Look! there's a snake!' or 'Danger!' or 'Be careful!'? By accumulation of experience, of course, he eventually reaches a reliable conclusion as to the 'correct' translation of 'nyoka', but when there is no such visible stimulus, uncertainty may remain.

That there is no one-to-one relationship between a fact and the language used to express it is perhaps illustrated by the following account. Two groups of patients suffering from the same illness were asked to locate the primary source of their illness and to say how much pain or other effects they suffered. One group was Italian, the other Irish.

'The groups described the effect of the same illness differently. Generally, the Irish described a specific dysfunction with limited bodily effects, while the Italians spoke of a diffuse disability, listing more kinds of dysfunction. The Irish tended to deny that their ailments affected them temperamentally, while the Italians scored high on an irritability scale. Zola suggests that the Italian, by overstating and dramatising his illness, hopes to dissipate the problem; whereas the Irishman, seeing life as full of privations, understates problems, as a defence mechanism. The author concludes that ethnicity may, therefore, be an important variable in preliminary diagnoses, since it affects the patient's recognition and communication of symptoms, and symptom-based health campaigns cannot assume that symptoms are objective facts.'[1]

Different people view the same objective facts in different ways, and express their perceptions in quite different language forms. The dramatic and understated reactions referred to above will be expressed in different linguistic terms, and no doubt if taped extracts of the discussions with the doctors were available these would show examples of the reflection in language of these varying attitudes to life. It is possible also to wonder to what extent the availability to these particular people of specific forms of language would influence their descriptions of their own illnesses. How do you, without gesture or excessive long-windedness, describe a pain in the trachea if your language has no word for a trachea, or if you do not know the word? It has been suggested by some linguists that our view of the world is largely conditioned by our mother tongue, and although few linguists or psychologists now agree with the unmodified theory, it has had considerable influence on thinking about the relationship of language to the people who use it. Few would deny that to some extent our views are coloured by the language readily at our disposal. But much more important for most of us, is the reverse process; not the extent to which our native language governs our lives, but the extent to which we control that language; the ranges and varieties of structure and words that we use, the intricacy of the patterns we master and understand. Modern research is beginning to find evidence for what has often been intuitively recognised, namely that the

1. *New Scientist*, 2nd February, 1967.

more flexible and wide-ranging a person's language is, the richer is likely to be the quality of his life. Conversely, the more restricted and limited his language, the more restricted and limited may be his life. If this is true, there would seem to be ample justification for more and more research to be done into language, its functions and its mechanisms, and how we master and employ it.

Language is greater than the sum of its parts, and it would be wrong to discuss the parts and mechanisms of language without a wider view of its functions. In this chapter I have tred to look at language as a whole by looking at some of the ways it is used by people. What has been said at some length can be said here in a much more precise form:

Language is used for:

    (i) phatic communion (i.e. as a social regulator);
    (ii) for ceremonial purposes;
    (iii) as an instrument of action;
    (iv) to keep the records;
    (v) to convey orders and information;
    (vi) to influence people;
    (vii) to enable self-expression;
    (viii) to embody or enable thought.

But the question 'What is Language?' still remains unanswered.

The answer will inevitably be complex, and if a listing of the uses of language helps to an understanding, it is still only a preliminary. In order to attempt an answer, it will be necessary to chop language up in rather arbitrary ways. Its complexities are such that it is virtually impossible to analyse it in any meaningful way without making these cuts. What sort of uses people put language to is a complex enough matter, how in fact language can be used to achieve these ends is more difficult to work out, and is a task for the specialist linguist, who also has to bear in mind the work of philosophers, psychologists and sociologists. The following chapters will attempt a preliminary look at some of the ways in which language achieves what people want of it. Language does so in no simple way, but by means of an interrelating series of different systems —systems of sounds, systems of grammatical patterning, systems of word meanings, systems of reference to non-linguistic events, all in turn combined and closely enmeshed in larger systems. To see the workings with any clarity it is necessary to take each of these systems in turn and examine it individually before it is possible to see how it interrelates with the others. And even with some insight into the different systems, or 'levels' as they are sometimes called, it is still necessary to choose some relatively arbitrary way of describing the relationship of these systems to each other. But if language is dismembered in this way, it must be remembered that the dismemberment is purely for convenience, for the different levels of language we choose to distinguish are of no validity unless they are set in the general framework of all the interrelating systems. So an anatomist may describe a human arm, or leg, or even a living human heart, but he cannot say anything really meaningful about it except in relation to the living, whole, body.

2

Spoken and Written Language

The old tradition of identifying 'book learning' with 'education' takes a long time to die, even if 'book learning' goes under some other name such as 'O' or 'A' levels. For most people, education is still equivalent to a mastery of the contents of books. Since education, at least in theory, enjoys high social status, the contents of books tend also to enjoy equal social status, and in far too many cases to be accepted wholly uncritically. 'What the book says . . .' may be regarded by people in less literate societies as definitive, and even in our own society is often generally accepted as probably right. This attitude is perhaps beginning to be paralleled by an acceptance of 'It said on the telly . . .' but even now the written word tends to carry more conviction than the spoken. Until recent years all study of language, in conformity with the generally accepted ideas of their relative merit, was based on the written rather than the spoken word. Where speech differed from writing, the usual attitude was, and often still is, that the speech was 'slovenly' or 'careless'. The feeling that 'good' speech should conform to 'good' writing was drummed into most of us, consciously or unconsciously, from early childhood. In fact the relationship between speech and writing is not so simple or easy, for they are by no means identical.

Most linguists now prefer to study the spoken forms of the language, basing their decision to do so on good grounds. They argue that the oral approach is justified, firstly, by the fact that historically it is evident that speech must have preceded writing. While the earliest form of writing known dates from about 3300 B.C. archaeological and other evidence suggests much earlier civilisations which would be inconceivable without a sophisticated form of language to establish and maintain them. The obvious fact of well-organised societies without written language is still a visible one in those many areas of the world today where a highly developed language has even now not yet been committed to paper, and yet where varying degrees of civilisation are quite adequately maintained without any form of writing. Therefore, the linguists will argue, writing must have been an attempt to represent the language that was spoken.

The chronological primacy of speech is therefore established. It is then argued that amendments to the written form of the language must in general have followed developments in the spoken form, though it may be recognised that occasionally this might not be true, as for instance with 'etymological' spelling where 'reforms' of spelling were introduced, not in order to reflect speech habits, for in fact they often contradicted them, but to show the 'origin' of the word. If one wishes then, to study language, it is logical to go to the primary source, i.e. spoken language, rather than to the derived, secondary source, such as writing represents, and which, moreover, is a 'language' only to a minority of the world's population.

While the justification for the oral approach is fully accepted, it should not be forgotten that in the more advanced civilisations at least, where a highly developed written language is in daily use by millions of people, even if purely passively, for example, in the reading of the newspapers, there are likely to be developments in written language which are not preceded by, or even paralleled by, developments in the spoken language. Literature is the obvious and perhaps the most important category; scientific and legal writing are others. Some literature, some scientific and legal writing, is based on oral language, but much more is not, and has developed forms which are highly esoteric in so far as relationship with the spoken language is concerned.

Further, in these cases, there are likely to be circumstances in which independent developments in written language do have an influence, if only in minor ways, on spoken language. Examples are the adoption into popular speech of such neologisms as 'chortle' and 'galumph' from writings by Lewis Carroll, or of words derived from written initials, such as UNESCO. Again, anyone listening to young children playing may hear forms of speech which can be traced, not to what they have

15

heard, but to what they have read in comics. Examples are 'Pow' and 'Zap' from the 'Batman' series, translated into a child's 'I'll pow you if you touch my bike'. These show signs of passing into adult language too, as a letter of 28th January, 1968, in *The Sunday Times* shows: 'It is fortunate that "the other side" lacks the sort of pragmatic, non-ideological, hard-headed realism that Mr Alsop represents. Else they might discern a hostile and pernicious tendency in North America and try to zap it out of existence.' Whether the writer would use 'zap' orally too one does not know, but it would seem likely. In the case of the children's use of such words we have a speech form derived from an artificial written form invented by journalists who produce comics.

In most circumstances therefore, and especially in places where language is used in ways that most concern us, i.e. in the 'advanced' civilisations, we have to recognise that there are two major independent forms of the 'same' language—the written and the spoken—which are alike in many aspects, but which have independent and possibly mutually influential characteristics. Within each of these **modes,** as it is convenient to call them, there are of course many other varieties of form, but these will be discussed more fully in Chapter 7.

In English (though by no means in the same measure in all languages), speech has one great resource denied to writing, namely the use of stress and intonation to convey meaning. On the other hand, writing has at its disposal a great many items which never normally find their way into speech, except where possibly speech consists of reading, which is a composite mode. Some words or phrases, for various reasons, practically never occur in impromptu speech, e.g. 'heretofore', which will only be found in certain kinds of writing and 'whom', which may possibly appear in the speech of older people but is now rare except in writing. Words like 'anti-sabbatarian' may appear in writing but are likely to be changed into something more familiar in speech; 'alight here for . . .' is notice-board English, almost certainly changed by the passenger to 'get out here for . . .' in his conversation with his fellow-passenger. This is not to say that these items cannot occur in speech, for all words can, and probably do, but to a greater or lesser extent they will seem to belong more 'naturally' to the written mode. Equally, certain structures are more at home in the written than the spoken mode, e.g. 'Passengers are requested to refrain from smoking', *or* 'There being no other nomination, Mr. Smith was duly elected.' The realisation in official quarters that the distance between the spoken and written forms has in some cases become so wide as to hinder the understanding of the public has resulted in the increasing tendency to reword notices such as 'Passengers are requested to refrain from smoking' to a simple 'No Smoking' or even 'Don't smoke'.

The attempt to represent speech in writing is an interesting study, particularly when the representation is compared with actual speech. A literal transcript of speech into the dialogue of a novel would probably appear quite unacceptable except over short stretches. When it is said that such-and-such an author has 'a good ear' for either 'dialogue' or the 'rhythms of native speech' or some such phrase, it is only rarely that what the author writes will in fact truly echo actual speech. 'Good' dialogue in the written form is mostly 'representational' rather than 'photographic', and 'good' can justly be applied to quite different approaches to the problem of representing speech in writing. Compare, for instance, the following:

(*a*) 'Santiago,' the boy said.
　　'Yes,' the old man said. He was holding his glass and thinking of many years ago.
　　'Can I go out and get sardines for you tomorrow?'
　　'No. Go and play baseball. I can still row and Rogelio will throw the net.'
　　'I would like to go. If I cannot fish with you, I would like to serve in some way.'
　　'You bought me a beer,' the old man said. 'You are already a man.'
　　'How old was I when you first took me in a boat?'
　　'Five, and you nearly were killed when I brought the fish in too green and he nearly tore the boat to pieces. Can you remember?'

'I can remember the tail slapping and banging and the thwart breaking and the noise of the clubbing. I can remember you throwing me into the bow where the wet coiled lines were and feeling the whole boat shiver and the noise of you clubbing him like chopping a tree down and the sweet blood smell all over me.'

'Can you really remember that or did I just tell it to you?'

'I remember everything from when we first went together.'

Ernest Hemingway, *The Old Man and the Sea*

(*b*) 'What did ye come away from yer own country for, young maister, if ye be so wownded about it?' inquired Christopher Coney, from the background, with the tone of a man who preferred the original subject. 'Faith, it wasn't worth your while on our account, for, as Maister Billy Wills says, we be bruckle folk here—the best o' us hardly honest sometimes, what with hard winters, and so many mouths to fill, and God-a'mighty sending his little taties so terrible small to fill 'em with. We don't think about flowers and fair faces, not we—except in the shape o' cauliflowers and pigs' chaps.'

'But no!' said Donald Farfrae, gazing round into their faces with honest concern; 'the best of ye hardly honest—not that surely? None of ye has been stealing what didn't belong to him?'

'Lord! no, no!' said Solomon Longways, smiling grimly. 'That's only his random way o' speaking. 'A was always such a man of under-thoughts' (And reprovingly towards Christopher): 'Don't ye be so over-familiar with a gentleman that ye know nothing of—and that's travelled a'most from the North Pole.'

Christopher Coney was silenced, and as he could get no public sympathy, he mumbled his feelings to himself; 'Be dazed, if I loved my country half as well as the young feller do, I'd live by claning my neighbour's pigsties afore I'd go away! For my part I've no more love for my country than I have for Botany Bay!'

Thomas Hardy, *The Mayor of Casterbridge*

Both of these passages could quite legitimately be held up as examples of 'good' dialogue writing, but the techniques have little in common with each other. To attempt an analysis of the differences would not be appropriate here, but what they have in common is that neither of them would be particularly close to a tape-recorded version of any 'live' conversation in such circumstances. Actual speech transcriptions, in phonetic notation, would no doubt show a number of features not represented in Hemingway's or Hardy's versions of dialogue—hesitations, repetitions, half-formed sentences and other features which are a normal part of most speech but which are usually excluded from written representations of speech. Above all, the conventional graphic markings, such as punctuation devices, can only very crudely suggest the stress and intonation patterns in the voice.

The conventional graphic markings do, however, give some indication of speech patterns. Question marks, exclamation marks, italics, underlining, paragraphing, dots to represent hesitations or unfinished utterances, all these are devices which, together with what one might call 'stage directions', such as 'he hesitated' or 'he said sharply' or 'he said questioningly', and so on, give some indication of voice patterns. In consecutive writing we are, moreover, rarely left in doubt as to the approximate intonation, since the context will normally give us adequate information. While the words 'Really' or 'Yes' on their own are barely intelligible, given a context which will determine their intonation, they can convey considerable information. When spoken language is considered in more technical detail in the next chapter, it will be easier to compare true speech with representations in literature of speech, because there will be available the technical means of doing so, but meanwhile here is one practical comment on the problem:

(c) 'But to read as if you were talking. Isn't that a trick?' 'Oh no, that's an art—or a craft, whichever you like. And in every art or craft there's a technique, a method, a way. What is it here? Well, I suppose each has to find his own; but my notion is that to read as if you were talking you must first write as if you were talking. What you have on the paper in front of you must be talk-stuff, not book-stuff.

'It's in part, a mere matter of how you put the words down on the paper. That very sentence now, the one you've just heard. It began with "It's in part . . ." If I'd said to you "It is, in part", you'd have thought, "He's reading". In speech we say "It's" not "It is". So we write "I T apostrophe S" and not "It is" on the paper. I know if I wrote "It is" I should say "It is" . . .

'I don't know anything about others, as I say, but my way is to speak my sentences aloud as I write them. In fact here's my second rule, all pat: "To write as you would talk you must talk while you write." If you were outside my room while I'm writing a talk you'd hear muttering and mumbling and outright declaration from beginning to end. You'd say, "There's somebody in there with a slate loose; he never stops talking to himself." No, I wouldn't be talking to *myself* but to you.'

J. Hilton, Oxford Book of English Talk

The question of how to represent spoken language exactly has been a problem over many centuries, and one which is even now not wholly solved, though some modern systems of phonetic transcription come perhaps nearer to it than ever before. For most ordinary purposes the use of the alphabet in the way conventionally accepted by any particular language is adequate, and the alphabet itself is indeed the culmination of many thousands of years of development of writing systems.

Before the alphabet, however, there were other systems of recording visual messages. Visual communication was in some places quite highly developed, so that there were relatively elaborate ways of marking trees, using smoke signals, knotted cords, and so on, which symbolically and visually conveyed messages otherwise conveyed only by word of mouth. This form of language must, one feels, have been restricted to the passing of information and orders, and must have been useful only in an immediate context. The earliest form of writing in a sense nearer to our own, is probably that of the Sumerian civilisation, about 3300 B.C., which was originally pictographic but which later developed more advanced forms. The stages by which writing developed to something more like our own use of it, might be summarised as follows.

At the earliest stage, a message might be conveyed simply by the drawing of a picture. This can be 'interpreted' into any language and is therefore not a representation of speech. Many modern advertisements rely largely on this sort of message, so that similar advertisements can be used right across the world. Few, however, dispense entirely with words. From this use of simple pictures, the next stage was to simplify and conventionalise the pictures so that a circle might come to represent the sun, or a picture of a man might be reduced to a shape suggesting only remotely a body, head and legs. Sometimes the symbols ceased to represent things, but came to be used to represent ideas, so that the circle comes to be not only the sun, but also heat, or light, or a god associated with the sun. This was then **ideographic** writing, useful but still limited in what it could do.

It then seems that signs gradually came to be associated not with the thing or idea which they represented, but with the sound or group of sounds in the language which was used in speech to represent them, so that there was then a representation at least two stages away from the original.

Thing   Speech representation   Written representation
Idea ⟫→   (symbol)   ⟫→   (symbol)
(e.g. 'sun')

This now is writing representing speech sounds. The shape of such writing will no longer need to be related to the original concept and can become completely arbitrary—the 'sun' no longer has to be represented with a round shape, or 'man' with a bifurcated symbol.

At one stage symbols represented, not individual sounds but syllables, as does Japanese script even today. This was, however, cumbersome when languages developed words with two or more consonants in a single syllable. A word like 'fa-mi-ly' can easily be represented by a 'syllabic' alphabet, but a word like 'strength' with its clusters of consonants would have to turn every consonant into a syllable, thus producing something like 'se-te-re-ne- ge- the'. The development of the modern alphabet where symbols represent sounds is much more economical and adaptable, even when as in English a one-to-one correspondence between symbol and sound can no longer be assumed. In English the symbols 'ough' can for example represent a variety of different sounds, as in words like 'plough', 'through', 'enough', 'cough', 'although', 'fought', and 'borough'.

Once alphabetic writing is achieved, the written language becomes a very flexible instrument, and as has been pointed out earlier, can achieve a life of its own, to some degree independent of speech. The extent to which written language influences the lives of millions of people is incalculable; it was probably the written language, at least after the invention of cheap and efficient printing processes, that did most to spread such ideas as Christianity and later, Marxism, so far and so fast. But the preoccupation in more recent times with 'personal contact' shows a realisation of the sometimes distorting and restricting effect of the written language. Industrial relations and trade union officials realise, or ought to realise, that speech is often clearer and more effective than printed notices; businessmen are now exhorted to talk to their customers abroad rather than merely to write to them; heads of large states maintain 'hot' lines which ensure that they can speak to each other as well as cable or write to each other. In these and many other ways we are coming back to a realisation of the importance of talk and to the achieving of a better balance between the degree of respect accorded to the written and spoken forms of the language.

3

The Sounds of Language (1)

Chapters 3 and 4 contain introductory matter to a study of phonetics. Even at this stage, it would be very helpful to have a teacher to give oral demonstration of points made. For any more detailed study, it would be essential.

In Chapter 2 it was said that a modern phonetic transcription was the best way to represent the exact sounds of speech. To be truly accurate, such a transcription has to be **narrow**, showing sound differences in great and rather cumbersome detail. Such a narrow transcription is, however, unnecessary for most non-technical purposes. But an ability to handle a less detailed, **broad** transcription, and even more, a knowledge of the principles underlying such transcription, is very useful, especially for language teachers.

Some knowledge of these principles, for instance, would give the teacher, or learner, an approach to the question of what constitutes a 'good accent'. In order to analyse why an Englishman speaking French almost always betrays the fact that he is English, by his English accent, or to be able to say what the difference is between a British English and an American English accent, it is necessary to study with some precision the actual noises the Englishman makes when he speaks French, or the American when he speaks English, and to work out why these noises are the same, and yet different, from the Frenchman's French and the Englishman's English.

The sounds of a language can be broken down and analysed in different ways, and their nature studied as they occur alone and in juxtaposition with others. The study of the actual sounds of language is called **phonetics** and the way in which these sounds are used, put together and organised in any one language is called **phonology** (or more usually **phonemics** in America). See if the distinction between a phonetic and a

23

phonemic study becomes clear by trying the following experiment. Say aloud the word 'tea'. Now try saying it in as many different ways as possible simply by moving the tip of the tongue farther and farther back in your mouth, by putting it between your teeth, by sticking it right out, and so on. You should be able to make a great variety of noises, recognisably different from each other, but also recognisably the same to anyone who assumes you are speaking English. Try saying even the most extreme form in a shop, and you'll probably still get your packet of tea leaves. If, however, you say 'dea' in any fashion, the shopkeeper is more likely to say something like 'What did you say, dear?', or simply to look puzzled. Phonetics will be able to describe the difference in the sounds of each of the variants of 'tea' and where they are different from 'dea', while phonology will account for the fact that in some respect, all the 'tea' sounds are the same, while the 'dea' sounds are in some way different enough to produce different results.

The differences between these 't' and 'd' sounds are differences of **segmental phonemes.** In the kind of English known as **Received Pronunciation**, that is, the kind of English most commonly spoken by educated people who do not have a regional accent (see p. 104), there are, for most people, twenty vowel phonemes, and twenty-four consonant phonemes. It is possible to make a different analysis of English which would yield different results, especially in so far as the vowels are concerned, for vowels vary considerably according to the part of the country and the social class to which the speaker belongs.

But in addition to these segmental phonemes, there are other elements which differentiate one utterance from another. These are the differences in sound which you will make when saying 'Really?' (doubtfully), 'Really!' (surprised) or 'Really!' (crossly). If you go back to the shop and ask for 'A pound of tea?' in the way in which you would normally ask a question, the shopkeeper is not likely to give it to you, but to look astonished that you should doubt his having any. In order to be intelligible, not only must a speaker make the distinction between 't' and 'd' sounds clear, but has also to make sure his voice goes up and down in the right places, and it is his success or failure in doing this which more than anything perhaps betrays his native or foreign origin.

Although both types of analysis are equally important, it is convenient when studying the sounds of language, to look at the segmental phonemes first. This chapter will go on to look at some of the general points about the production of noises we call speech, and then examine the ways in which these can be classified, with particular reference to English sounds. In Chapter 4 the more elusive non-segmental differences will be looked at, again with particular reference to English.

There are a number of different stages at which it is possible to study language sounds. It is possible to study the sounds as they are received and interpreted in the hearer's ear (**auditory phonetics**), or to study the actual sound waves and their characteristics (**acoustic phonetics**) or finally to study the way in which the sounds are produced in the speaker's body (**articulatory phonetics**). Acoustic phonetics is of great use to telecommunications engineers and others, but it is a relatively new and undeveloped study, as yet of little practical use to language learners or teachers. For their purpose, articulatory (and to a lesser degree auditory) phonetics supplies the most useful field of study. The actual production of speech sounds, though even yet by no means an exact study, can be described and hence analysed and copied, or compared, with a useful degree of precision.

In order to attempt a description, it is necessary to know the basic mechanisms by which speech—any speech—is uttered. None of the bodily organs seems to be primarily designed for speech, but a number of organs which have other primary uses, have as a secondary use, the production of speech. The lungs, throat, mouth and nose are the obvious locations of the sources of sound, and the production of most speech sounds can be traced by following the air stream through these parts of the body. The air stream which is used to produce most English

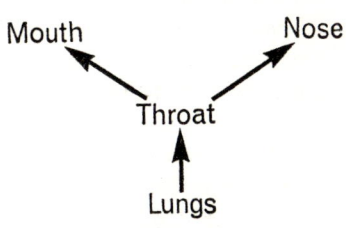

sounds is that expelled from the lungs; in some languages the air is utilised as it is drawn in for some sounds.

Some kinds of stammering produce sounds which are made with an indrawn supply of air, and even those of us who do not stammer will occasionally, if surprised or afflicted by a sudden sharp pain, produce a sound by sharply drawing breath in. We can, in English, also make some significant sounds without using an air stream at all—for instance, the sound conventionally represented as 'tut-tut', in disapproval, or the sound made to encourage a horse, but these minor exceptions apart, all English speech sounds use air passing out from the lungs.

VOWELS AND CONSONANTS

If you open your mouth as widely as possible, allow the air to escape freely, and emit continuous sound—try it—you will produce a **vowel**. If the shape of your mouth is then altered by moving the lips and jaw, while still keeping the lips apart, a number of different vowels are produced. If the mouth is still kept open, but its shape altered by moving the lips and the tongue, making the tongue higher or lower in the mouth, further variations of the vowels will be produced, some of them recognisably English sounds, others perhaps reminiscent of vowel sounds heard in other languages, and others simply 'noise'. Once again, phonetics will be able to describe all the sounds you have made in the course of doing this, phonology will isolate those sounds which are used in any one language, such as English, and describe how they are used, where they contrast with one another, what range of sound can in that language reasonably be described as belonging to one 'vowel', and so on. Phonology will be able to account for the fact that although the Londoner and the Lancastrian probably say 'glass' in two quite different ways, no English person has any difficulty in deciding that they are both talking about the same thing.

When you were opening your mouth and saying 'Ah', and then trying all the variants made by moving lips and tongue, you probably found that in order to allow the air to escape freely and to make continuous sounds as you were asked to do, you had to take care that your tongue did not get too close to any other part of the mouth such as the teeth, or roof of the mouth. If, in fact, any part of the tongue did approach a part of the mouth so as either to block the air stream, or to cause friction as the air stream was forced through the gap, you would have made a **consonant**. (For partial exceptions see below.) The main difference, phonetically speaking, between a vowel and a consonant is that, in making a consonant, the air stream through the mouth is at some point either blocked, or partially obstructed, while in making a vowel the air escapes unrestricted. By and large there is no great difficulty in reconciling this with the commonly accepted idea of vowel and consonant, though you may find that whereas you are accustomed to calling / l / and / r / consonants, they seem to have more of the characteristics of vowels in the sense in which we have been discussing the differences. The traditional definition of vowel and consonant has been based on the fact that 'vowels' are usually the nuclear, or central element in a syllable (or can form an entire syllable on their own), while a 'consonant' has been a marginal component, usually associated with the beginning or ending of a syllable. This distinction is usually referred to as a 'linguistic' definition of a vowel or consonant, whereas the distinction between the open or obstructed air stream is a 'phonetic' one.

NOTATION

In order to describe sounds, it is customary to use a form of notation which can give a description both more accurate and more economical than to attempt to do so by ordinary alphabetical resources. Thus if you want to describe the vowel sound in 'late' it is inadequate to use 'a', since 'a' in 'mat' represents quite a different sound. Moreover the vowel sound in 'late' can also be represented in spelling by ai (waist), ay (day), ei (eight), ey (they), ea (great) and ê (fête). To have to say the 'the sound "a" as in "late" ' every time you wanted to refer to it would not only be clumsy, but misleading or useless to a foreigner learning English. There are, however, various notations where a symbol represents a sound rather than a spelling. Of the different phonetic notations available, the best known is perhaps that of the International Phonetic Association. The I.P.A. symbols which are most useful to represent English vowel sounds are:

i e ɛ ə ɜ æ ɔ ʌ u ʊ ɑ ɒ

and English also needs to combine some of them to represent English **diphthongs** (that is vowel sounds which are composed of two sound elements). To represent English vowel phonemes (see below), we use therefore:

English short vowels	English long vowels	Diphthongs
/ i / as in sit	/ i: / as in see	/ ei / as in fail
/ e / as in get	/ u: / as in fool	/ ɑi / as in hide
/ æ / as in man	/ ɑ: / as in heart	/ ɔi / as in foil
/ ɔ / as in hot	/ ɔ: / as in awe	/ əu / as in go
/ u / as in book	/ ə: / as in heard	/ ɑu / as in how
/ ʌ / as in bud	(: indicates length)	/ iə / as in here
/ ə / as in *a*go or		/ ɛə / as in there
China		/ uə / as in tour

For English consonants the following symbols are used:

/ b / as in bin	/ d / as in din	/ k / as in cot
/ p / as in pin	/ t / as in tin	/ g / as in got
/ f / as in fat	/ θ / as in thigh	/ s / as in sin
/ v / as in vat	/ ð / as in thy	/ z / as in zoo
/ ʃ / as in shoe	/ h / as in head	/ dʒ / as in gin
/ ʒ / as in lei*s*ure		/ tʃ / chin
/ m / as in man	/ l / as in led	/ j / as yet
/ n / as in net	/ r / as in red	/ w / as in wet
/ ŋ / as in sang		

Symbols also, of course, exist for non-English sounds, such as ø for the French vowel in 'deux' and β for the Spanish sound in 'haber'. These will be explained and used as necessary.

Symbols which are used phonetically, i.e. those which describe as accurately as possible a sound, are usually written between square brackets [ ]; when the symbols represent the phonemes of a particular language, as when they are used to represent the English sounds above, they are written between slants / /. Let us look again, a little more closely, at what we mean by a phoneme.

THE PHONEME

You will see that in the list of symbols given above, only one symbol is given for all the sounds you could make at the beginning of the word 'tea' which would still ensure your getting the appropriate commodity. Similarly 'book' is shown as having the symbol 'u' to represent its vowel, even though people you know may actually say it in a number of different ways, depending on where they come from and their own personal speech habits. The variations in the way 'tea' or 'book' are said are not sufficient to make a difference to the meaning of the words, whereas a slight difference in the vibration of the vocal cords and slightly less air escaping from the mouth between the 't' and the 'ea' sounds will result in 'dea' and perplexity to the shopkeeper. When the difference in sound between two ways of saying something results in a change of meaning, the articulation has moved to a different phoneme; in other words, in English the difference between 'tin' and 'din' is **phonemic**, whereas the difference between 'tea' with the tongue tip on your teeth (as the French might say it) and 'tea' with the tongue tip on the ridge behind the teeth (as the English usually say it) is **phonetic**. The sounds symbolised in the list above are the sounds which are phonemic in English; to change from one of the symbols to another in a word would change the meaning of the word. For languages other than English, the list would have to be different. For instance, other languages recognise the difference between two, or even three of the / k / sounds which an Englishman uses in '*k*eep *c*alm and *c*ool' / ki:p ka:m n ku:l /. The English person normally has to be specially trained even to hear the difference in these three

29

/ k / sounds whereas, to the Arab, the fact that the / k / sound is made either further forward or further back in the mouth is significant enough to result in a possible change of meaning. Some sounds in English sound very different to English speakers, so that for instance no native speaker would ever confuse 'lot' and 'rot', but to many speakers of African languages in which the difference between / l / and / r / is not phonemic, they sound exactly the same. One of my students in Africa, for instance, was called Veronica or Velonica indifferently by her fellow students, who failed to understand why I should ask whether it was Veronica or Velonica, since to them I was repeating the same name.

A phoneme then is the smallest unit of sound by means of which a change of meaning can be effected in any one language. Phonemes are identified for a language by setting up a series of contrasting pairs of words and showing that by altering the sound at any one point the meaning is altered. This is the means whereby the list on page 28 was established.

Before describing in more detail the English vowel and consonant phonemes, it is as well to master some terminology which will make description easier. This is mainly concerned with the bodily means of articulating sounds.

ARTICULATION

Men (and animals) produce sounds by utilising the mechanisms of certain organs of the body, chiefly the lungs, throat, mouth and nose. The variations in sound are achieved partly by varying the position of the lips and tongue in relation to the teeth, alveolar ridge, hard and soft palate and occasionally the uvula. Different parts of the tongue are used for different purposes, and are distinguished as the tip, blade, front and back of the tongue. The vocal cords are also used in different ways. Let us look at each of these parts in closer detail.

(*a*) *Lips*   These are used in a number of ways. By altering their shape from rounded to spread, by protruding or retracting them, considerable variation is made in the shape of the interior of the mouth (the oral cavity), and the resonance of a sound produced will vary accordingly. French makes considerable use of the distinction between spread and rounded lips in forming vowels. Compare for instance the vowel sounds in 'deux' and 'dé' where the main, though not the only, difference lies in the spreading or rounding of the lips. English tends to make less wide variations of lip position, but in making English vowels the phoneticians distinguish between lips which are **neutral** (position as in 'get'), **spread** (as in 'see'), **open** (as in 'card'), **close rounded** (as in 'do') and **open rounded** (as in 'got').

In making the English consonants / p / / b / / m / the lips are closed, thus either deflecting the air through the nose (as in / m /) or blocking it and then releasing it (as in / p / and / b /). In making / f / and / v / the lower lip and teeth are used. In languages such as Spanish there is a further position where the lips are close enough together so that friction occurs when air is expelled through them. The word **labial** is used to refer to lip position.

(*b*) *Teeth* The teeth, in combination with other organs such as lips or tongue, are used to make certain consonants such as / f / / v / / l / / n / or sometimes / r /, or in French / t / and / d /. Details of how these sounds are made will be found in the section on English consonants. They are referred to as **dental** sounds.

(*c*) *Alveolar Ridge* This is the ridge which can be felt just behind the upper front teeth. As with the teeth, the tongue, in contact with the alveolar ridge gives an articulatory position which results, with other factors, in the production of consonants such as / s / in 'sell' / z / in 'zoo' or the sound in '*sh*oe' or 'plea*s*ure'. The word **alveolar** is used to refer to positions involving this ridge.

(*d*) *Soft Palate* The shifting of parts of the tongue in relation
(*e*) *Hard Palate* to the roof of the mouth is one of the principal
(*f*) *Nasal Cavity* ways of producing a variety of vowels. The hard
palate—the roof of the mouth—is fixed; the

31

soft palate—the part of the roof much nearer the back of the mouth—has a certain amount of freedom of movement, though it is difficult to feel this. It can be raised or lowered; when it is in the raised position the nasal passage is blocked and air can escape through the mouth only. When it is in the lowered position, air can escape through mouth and nose unless the mouth is blocked in some other way, such as by the lips when they close to make / m /, or by the tongue making an obstruction with the alveolar ridge in making / n /. Most English sounds are made with the soft palate raised, air escaping through the mouth only; the 'nasal' English sounds / m / / n / and / ŋ / as in 'sum' / sʌm / 'sun' / sʌn / and 'sung' / sʌŋ / are made with the soft palate lowered, but with the mouth blocked at the lips, alveolar ridge or palate respectively; the French nasal vowels are made with the soft palate lowered and the mouth unobstructed so that air escapes through mouth and nose.

If the passage into the nose is blocked, as for instance with a heavy cold, the 'nasal' consonants / m / / n / and / ŋ / cannot be made with the air passing through the nasal cavity, and since the mouth cavity will be blocked by the attempt at articulating, no sound can be produced. Since the nasal cavity cannot be unblocked, we have to release the mouth cavity, and the oral equivalents of the nasal consonants are produced so that 'morning' / mɔ:niŋ / becomes / bɔ:dig /.

To refer to the soft palate the term **velar** is used, for the hard palate **palatal**, and in reference to the nasal cavity, **nasal**.

(*g*) *Uvula* This is the small appendage at the end of the velum or soft palate. It can be seen quite clearly by looking in a mirror. Not a great deal of use is made of the uvula in English speech, but the most usual French / r / sound nowadays is made by friction between the back of the tongue and the uvula. It is more often used in some Eastern languages.

(*h*) *Tongue* The tongue is by far the most versatile and useful of the articulatory organs, a fact long recognized in the fairly common use of the word 'tongue' as equivalent to 'language'. 'The Treasure of our Tongue' is a recently published book; our 'mother tongue' has many sentimental as well as practical overtones. **Lingual** is sometimes used to refer to tongue positions.

As has already become evident in the descriptions so far given, the position of the tongue is the most important factor in the distinguishing of the various vowel sounds. It is very difficult to feel the movements of the tongue when it is not in actual contact with the other parts of the mouth, and judgements of vowel quality therefore usually have to be made by listening to the sounds and varying the position by aural judgements. This does not alter the fact that the variations, between for instance / i: / in 'see' and / æ / in 'man', are made by adjusting movements of the tongue. There are now various techniques, such as X-ray photography, for ascertaining tongue positions, but for the most part, the teaching of the appropriate vowel sounds for any language will have to be by mimicry and aural training. It is nevertheless useful for a language teacher to be aware of the mechanism of vowel production, especially when it comes to comparison of similar sounds in different languages. To compare for instance the English / i: / in 'see' with the French / i / in 'lit', it is useful to be able to analyse the difference in terms of tongue position. This will be dealt with more fully later. The various parts of the tongue need to be distinguished: the **tip**, which is self-explanatory; the **blade**, which is a small area immediately behind the tip; the **front** of the tongue, which rather misleadingly means what common sense might call the middle, i.e. that part behind the blade and before the back; and the **back**, which is the furthermost part of the tongue away from the tip. As has been seen, many consonants are also formed by the tongue coming into contact with other parts of the mouth.

(i) Vocal Cords The air coming up from the lungs passes through the larynx, the front part of which can be felt by putting the fingers on the 'Adam's apple' in the throat just below the chin. If you try keeping your fingers there while uttering a continuous sound 'z . . . z . . . z . . . z . . .' and then changing to a continuous sound 's . . . s . . . s . . . s . . .' you will feel a certain amount of

33

vibration during the / z / sound which ceases as you change to the / s / sound. If you try holding your fingers there while speaking normally but not too quickly you will feel the vibration starting or shutting off at various points. Inside the larynx are two folds of ligament and elastic tissue usually called the **vocal cords.** These cords can be brought together and closed, can be wide open, or can be so close together that they vibrate when air passes through them. The difference in sounds that these varying positions effect is used extensively in English to distinguish phonemes. Thus, one of the differences between / p / and / b /, / s / and / z /, / f / and / v / lies in the fact that the first member of each pair is **voiceless,** i.e. that the vocal cords do not vibrate, and the second of each pair is **voiced,** i.e. the vocal cords are vibrating. Although this is true of the sounds in isolation, however, it is not always true of sounds in particular parts of the word, or in a stream of speech. Again, one of the contrasts between English and French is that while / b / / d / / g / are not always voiced in English, they should always be voiced in French, so that an English person speaking French will have an 'English accent' if he ignores this fact. This and numbers of other relatively minor points are what in total constitute the difference between the native and the foreign speaker of a language. The unconscious articulatory habits of one's mother tongue are carried over to the new tongue, and without some phonetic awareness, or a highly developed ability to mimic, it is difficult to isolate and therefore to remedy the faulty articulation.

The opening between the vocal cords is called the **glottis**. If the glottis is tightly closed, lung air can be stopped behind it, or if it is held open in such a way as to impede, but not stop, the air stream, friction may be caused.

The **pitch** of a voice is altered by altering the rate of vibration of the vocal cords. Thus a very deep gruff voice will be the result of the cords vibrating very slowly, a high-pitched voice will mean that the vocal cords are vibrating at a more rapid rate. A man's vocal cords are likely to open and close 100–150 times a second when he is speaking in a normal voice, a woman's perhaps 200–325 times. The loudness and softness of a voice are also controlled here—by the size of the puff of air which escapes at each vibration (see also p. 50ff).

THE CARDINAL VOWEL SYSTEM

The difficulty of describing how a vowel is articulated in terms of how one feels the position of the articulatory organs has been mentioned earlier. In order to assist in the description of vowel sounds, Daniel Jones formulated the system known as the cardinal vowel system, which can be illustrated diagrammatically and which is very useful when attempting to contrast the vowels of different languages.

Vowels, as has been said, are differentiated largely by variations in tongue position. The main movements consist of the raising or lowering of either the front, or back, of the tongue. Thus the four most widely different vowels are:

(*a*) front of the tongue very high;
(*b*) front of the tongue very low;
(*c*) back of the tongue very low;
(*d*) back of the tongue very high.

Represented diagrammatically:

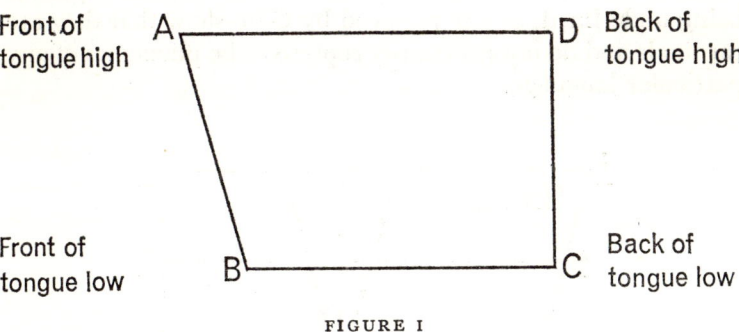

FIGURE I

The line A–B then represents the front of the tongue moving from the highest to the lowest part of the mouth, and line C–D represents the back of the tongue moving from the lowest to the highest point of the mouth. Line A–D and B–C will represent a

35

gradual change from the front to the back of the tongue. An imaginary point in the centre of this rectangle would represent the centre point of the tongue being half-way between the high and low positions. It is usual to call the positions of the tongue close and open, rather than high and low, and this will be adopted, so that now one can re-label this diagram, and add some further markings to indicate intermediate tongue positions.

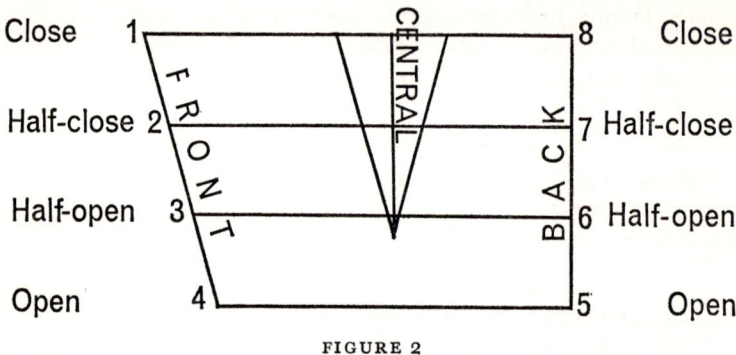

FIGURE 2

Points 1–8 on this diagram represent the primary cardinal vowels. These can be given phonetic notation, the symbols being underlined, or else prefaced by C, to show that they are cardinals and do not necessarily represent the phonemes of any particular language.

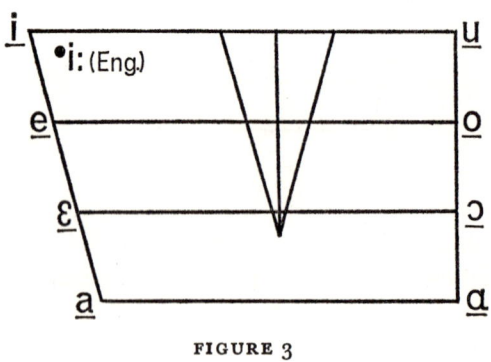

FIGURE 3

Vowels of any language can now be described with reference to this, so that for instance, French / i / in 'lit' can be said to equal the first cardinal, whereas English / i:/ in 'see' can be shown diagrammatically as slightly lower and more central. Anyone pronouncing French 'lit' with the front of the tongue lower, and the central part of the tongue rather higher than a French person normally would do will make a sound like the English 'see' vowel and will therefore be 'speaking French with an English accent'.

ENGLISH SOUNDS

Let us now look briefly at English sounds, using those sounds which are usually associated with what is called Received Pronunciation, that is, the kind of English which is recognised as the speech of educated persons who do not have a regional accent. The question of different kinds of English speech will be dealt with in more detail later in the book.

VOWELS

First of all, here are the long and short vowels which were listed on page 28 drawn in their approximate positions on the Cardinal vowel chart.

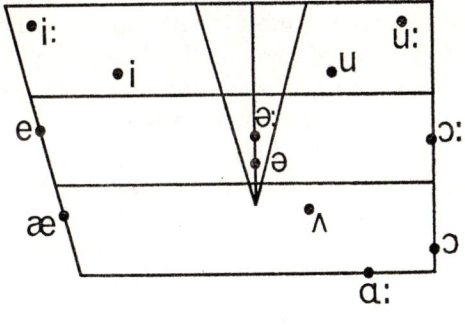

FIGURE 4

It will be seen that none of these vowels corresponds exactly to any of the cardinal vowels, in contrast to, for example,

37

French vowels, some of which are equivalent to cardinals. This diagram shows some of the French vowels.[1]

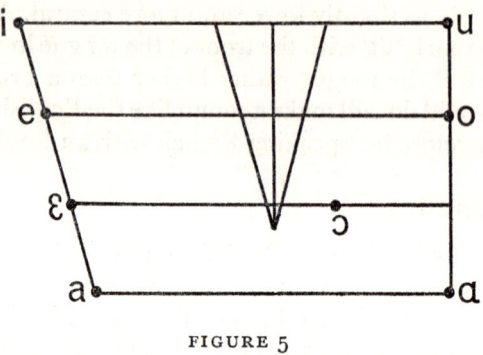

FIGURE 5

By drawing up inclusive charts of all English vowels and the vowels of another language, it is easy to see where one language has vowels that another lacks, or where similar vowels are in fact different, and this can be a useful aid to teaching.

DIPHTHONGS

The chart in Fig. 4 included only the short and long vowels of English. The remaining English vowel sounds you will notice are represented by two symbols / ei /, / ai /, etc. This is because they do in fact consist of two sounds, the voice gliding from one to another. Thus with / ei / the articulatory organs first take up the appropriate position to make a sound in the area of / e /, and then move approximately to the appropriate position for an / i / sound. This movement is indicated on the cardinal vowel chart by an arrow indicating the direction of the glide. The following diagrams show the English diphthongs. The pronunciation of many dialect speakers will be rather different from that shown here, but the more common variety of Received English pronunciation is approximately as shown:

1. Many French speakers do not have different vowels for / a / and / ɑ/, but use only one intermediate vowel. Modern treatments of French phonetics therefore may recognise only one vowel, which is neither cardinal 4 nor 5, but lies between the two.

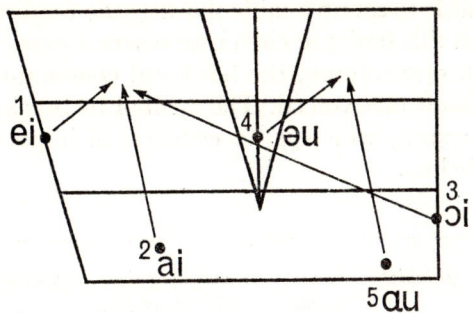

FIGURE 6

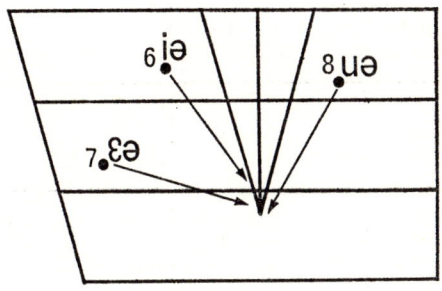

FIGURE 7

1. / ei / fail   ⎫
2. / ai / hide   ⎬ glide to / i / position.
3. / ɔi / foil   ⎭

4. / əu / go   ⎫ glide to / u / position
5. / au / how   ⎭

6. / iə / here   ⎫
7. / ɛə / there   ⎬ glide to ə position
8. / uə / tour   ⎭

CONSONANTS

Consonants are usually described by three main factors—(i) the point at which they are articulated; (ii) the way in which they are articulated; and (iii) whether they are voiced or not (i.e. whether the vocal cords vibrate or not).

39

It is possible to set up a table showing the English consonants classified on this basis; in each case where a pair of consonants is shown in one column, the left hand consonant is voiceless, the right hand one voiced. The symbol in brackets is a non-phonemic sound, which is nevertheless of importance and is described below.

	Bilabial	*labio-dental*	*dental and alveolar*	*palato-alveolar*	*palatal*	*velar*	*glottal*
Plosive	p b		t d			k g	(ʔ)
Nasal	m		n			ŋ	
Lateral (without friction)			l				
Fricatives		f v	θ ð s z	ʃ ʒ			h
Affricates				tʃ dʒ			
Continuants without friction and semi-vowels	w		r		j		

It is not possible here to give a full description of how all these sounds are made, but a brief account will indicate how the table is to be interpreted.

PLOSIVES (STOPS)

/ p / pin	/ t / tin	/ k / cot
/ b / bin	/ d / din	/ g / got

For all these sounds, the basic mechanism is that the air stream coming up from the lungs meets an obstruction, a complete closure, in the mouth, where the air is briefly held and then released with a degree of 'explosion'. The air is *stopped*, then *exploded*. In the case of / p / and / b / the stop is at the lips, which are closed, then opened to release the air—hence **bilabial plosives**. In the case of / t / and / d / the stop occurs at the point where the tongue tip rests on the alveolar ridge—hence **alveolar plosives**. With / k / and / g / the back of the tongue rests on the soft palate, forming a closure at the back of the mouth—therefore **velar plosives**. In making / p / / t / and / k / the vocal cords do not vibrate, whereas with / b / / d / and / g / they do.

The **glottal stop** / ʔ / is a very common sound in English, particularly in some regional dialects. Here the vocal cords are tightly closed, and then suddenly separated allowing the air to pass through. If you say 'reaction' or 'coordinate' slowly and carefully, the slight pause between the syllables 're-' and '-action' and 'co-' and '-ordinate' is likely to be in fact taken up by a glottal plosive. If you say 'yes!' with great emphasis, it is likely to be preceded by a glottal stop. Cockney speech traditionally uses a glottal stop in place of some of the other stops as in 'a bi*t* of bu*tt*er' or 'a cu*p* of tea'.

/ biʔə bʌ ʔ/   / ə kʌʔ ə təi /

NASALS / m / mat / n / not / ŋ / sing

The main characteristic of these sounds is that the air from the lungs passes out through the nose rather than the mouth. The blockage in the mouth occurs at the lips for / m /—'mat'—bilabial; at the alveolar ridge for / n /—'not'—alveolar; and on the soft palate for / ŋ /—'sing'—velar.

41

LATERAL   / l / ('leaf' or 'hill')

These sounds are so called because the air escapes at the sides of the tongue, the tip of which is usually resting on the centre of the teeth ridge. There is usually no friction as the air escapes, and the sounds are usually voiced. They are therefore rather like vowels, and for this reason can often behave in a word rather like a vowel. For instance, in 'apple' /æpl /, 'satchel' / sætʃl / and 'bottle' / bɔtl / the / l / sounds are syllabic.

Although they are not phonemically distinct it is worth noting that English uses three different [l] sounds. These three [l] sounds are called clear, [l], dark, [ɫ], and voiceless [l̥] If you say the word 'Lil' and listen carefully you will hear a slight difference in the two [l] sounds. It is also a useful exercise for other purposes, because by saying the two [l] sounds one after the other and trying to hear and feel the difference, you will gradually be able to feel the tongue movement, for the difference between the two [l] sounds in 'Lil' consists of the difference between the position of the front and back of the tongue. The first [l] sound is a clear one, made with the front of the tongue raised, the second, a dark [ɫ], has the back of the tongue raised, though in both cases the tip of the tongue remains anchored in the same position. Most English people use clear [l] before vowels and / j / and dark [ɫ] before a consonant, at the end of a word, after a vowel, and if it is used as a syllable.

The voiceless [l] sound [l̥] is made in some words such as 'please'. Here the vocal cords do not vibrate. When this happens it is a weak variety of the Welsh sound you may be familiar with and which is represented by the spelling 'll' in words such as 'Llandudno' or 'Llangollen'.

FRICATIVES   / f / fat   / θ / thigh   / s / sad   / ʃ / ship
              / v / vat   / ð / thy   / z / zoo   / ʒ / leisure
              / h / hot

In the case of all these sounds, the basic mechanism consists of the air from the lungs passing through the mouth, but at some point going through a gap between the articulatory organs so narrow that friction is caused as the air passes through. With the pair / f / and / v / the upper teeth and lower lip are lightly in contact, so that air escapes with friction between them; these are called the **labio-dental fricatives.**

With / θ / and / ð / tip and rims of the tongue touch the teeth very lightly and air escapes between the forward surface of the tongue and the teeth. Both these sounds are represented by 'th' in spelling, but the difference between them can be clearly heard if you compare 'mouth' and 'mouthe' / mauθ / and / mauð /, or the pair given above. These are referred to as the **dental fricatives.**

/ s / and / z / are the **alveolar fricatives.** As the name indicates, the friction here is caused by the tongue tip and blade lightly touching the alveolar ridge. The side rims of the tongue are firmly on the upper side teeth, but the tongue is grooved and the air escapes down this groove, and then with friction, between the tongue and the alveolar ridge.

/ ∫ / and / ʒ /. For these sounds the tip and blade of the tongue are near the alveolar ridge, and the front part of the tongue is raised towards the hard palate. The air escapes between the roof of the mouth and quite a large tongue area. These are called the **palato-alveolar fricatives.**

/ h /. This is here included as a **glottal fricative**, although the sound has some vowel-like qualities. It occurs in English only at the beginning of syllables and before vowels. The upper parts of the mouth and throat are in position ready for the following vowel and the actual sound of / h / varies according to the vowel which follows. In itself it consists of air expelled with considerable pressure through the open vocal cords, which are not vibrating.

AFFRICATES

These sounds have some of the characteristics of both stops and fricatives. In order to make them, a blockage is formed in the mouth as for plosives, but the air is then released, not with an explosion, as in / p / / b /, etc., but more slowly, with friction

43

occurring between the organs which made the blockage. The sound at the beginning and end of a word like 'church' or 'judge', for instance, consists of the air being first blocked as for / t / or / d /, then released with friction as in / ʃ / or / ʒ /. The friction is shorter than in the usual fricatives and it may be misleading to think of the affricates as / t / + / ʃ / and / d / + / ʒ / since the sound in 'church' or 'judge' is for all practical purposes *one sound* / ʧ / or / ʤ / often written as here, ligatured, but more often simply for ease or economy as / tʃ / and / dʒ /[1]

SEMI-VOWELS

You will perhaps when trying to classify the vowels and consonants find difficulty with the initial sounds in words like 'wet' and 'yet'. You may also have found difficulty in working out why in the face of the school 'rule' of 'a' before consonants and 'an' before vowels we still say 'a European' or 'a union' rather than 'an European' or 'an union'. The initial sound in 'you' is the same, if you listen closely, to the sound immediately following the initial consonant in 'cue'. Similarly the first sound in 'wick' is the same as the second sound in 'quick'. Thus we have:

you / juː/   cue / kjuː /   and also union / juːnjən /
wick / wik /   quick /kwik /   European / juərəpiːən /

We are accustomed to calling these sounds, represented by / j / and /w/, consonants, largely because they occur in typically consonantal positions in words, but phonetically they are nearer to a vowel glide. In saying 'yet' you will, if you listen carefully, hear that you are gliding rapidly from the vowel sound of / iː / (as in 'see') to the vowel represented by the second symbol / e / in / jet /. Similarly with 'wet' you are gliding rapidly from the / uː / position in 'fool' to the / e / of 'wet'.

These sounds then are called semi-vowels. / j / is technically, an **unrounded palatal semi-vowel** and / w / a **labio-velar semi-vowel**. In fact with / j / and / w/ , the actual position of the tongue and lips will depend very much on the nature of the

1. Some phoneticians will also classify / tr /   / dr /   / ts / and / dz / as affricates.

44

following sound, so that lips will be much more rounded for 'wood' / wud / than for 'wet' / wet /.

FRICTIONLESS CONTINUANT / r /

As with / j / and / w /, the English / r / sound, phonetically, may appear to be nearer to a vowel than to a consonant. Many different variations of the / r / sound are heard throughout the country, and between different speakers. The most common variety, however, is made without any stop or friction, and is therefore in many respects vowel-like. One point to watch in particular is that in many cases in English, the written language uses an 'r' symbol where no / r / sound is in fact made. In 'cart', for instance, only certain American, Scottish or other non-R.P. speakers use an / r / sound. For most speakers in this country 'cart' is pronounced / ka:t /, and 'horse' is / hɔ:s /. In words like 'there' or 'fear' the written 'r' symbol does not reflect the pronunciation, so that 'there' is / ðɛə / and 'fear' is / fiə /. The most common English / r / sound is made with the tip of the tongue near to the alveolar ridge, but not touching it. The rims of the back of the tongue touch the upper side teeth and the tongue generally is slightly hollowed so that air can escape easily, without any friction, over a large area.

This description of English sounds has of necessity been brief and sketchy, but should give some idea of how sounds are formed.

A more detailed account of the sounds of English, and the many variations, can be found in recent editions of Daniel Jones's 'The Pronunciation of English', or in A. C. Gimson's 'An Introduction to the Pronunciation of English', which, however, uses a slightly different transcription system.

4

The Sounds of Language (11)

STRESS AND INTONATION

It is at least possible to argue that when we listen to, and understand someone speaking to us, we understand almost as much from the way the voice goes up and down as we do from the actual combinations of vowels and consonants. Certainly a dog trained to respond to certain utterances will continue to respond if the vowels and consonants are slightly changed but all other factors kept constant. Many of us as children have played the game of talking without words—carrying on a fairly prolonged conversation of 'Mmm?' 'Mmmmmmmm!', and so on. Or we have listened to one end of a telephone conversation, the end audible to us consisting almost solely of grunts, or 'uh-hus', etc., and when the speaker finally puts down the telephone we are able to say, 'That didn't sound too good, what's the matter?' or 'Sounds as if that's all right then?', basing our interpretation on the voice patterns, rather than on any actual words. Again, the interpretation of a sentence such as 'John says Mary is a fool' will depend entirely on voice tunes to tell us whether it is John or Mary who is the fool. The voice tunes are sometimes partially represented in the written language by the presence or absence of punctuation: 'John, says Mary, is a fool' would be an alternative written interpretation. But the written language does not always offer even this help. In the written language, without further context, 'The dangerous medicine cupboard' could be either 'the cupboard in which dangerous medicines are kept' or 'the medicine cupboard which is dangerous (liable to collapse)', whereas the spoken language will almost invariably make enough distinction for the meaning to be quite clear. Similarly, 'He's a good workman, did you say?' is neutral in written language, but may carry a variety of meanings from

46

doubt or factual inquiry to incredulity, in the spoken language.

The two factors which give spoken language this greater flexibility are the factors of **stress** and **intonation**. They are far more complex in English than was realised until a relatively short time ago, and even the more comprehensive accounts now published are only partial and in some areas, doubtful descriptions. Nevertheless there are certain fundamental components of both stress and intonation which it is useful to know about.

STRESS

Technically, it is not easy to describe stress; practically, few native English speakers have difficulty in at least recognising it when they hear it, so that for instance they can tell you that in 'forget' the second syllable is stressed and in 'later' the first syllable is stressed. If asked to say how they know, most people will say that the relevant syllable is 'louder' than the other, and for present purposes this is perhaps enough. A stressed syllable in a word is therefore one that is heard as 'louder' than others. It should, however, be noted that this is not a wholly accurate account of word stress, merely a convenient 'shorthand' as an introduction to the subject. Using this, it is not difficult for the native speaker to mark the stressed syllables in isolated words as is shown below. (' is used immediately *before* the stressed syllable).

for'get 'happy 'better a'lone 'husband
or in longer words

unack'nowledged fas'tidious 'agonisingly
adminis'tration tele'vision (or would you mark it
'television?)

Apart from a few words like television, controversy ('controversy or con'troversy) where usage tends to vary, there is a 'normal' stress in each word, recognised and followed by all native speakers. As has been seen in these few examples, however, there is in English no one uniform place for the stress—it may be on the first, last, penultimate or indeed any syllable, so that if we meet an isolated new word with which we are quite

47

unfamiliar we are likely to be in difficulty over where to put the stress. For example, there is an advertisement which still perplexes me, which includes a name 'Cantrece'. ('/ kæntris/? /kæn'tri:tʃ/? or/kæntri:'tʃe/?) And should 'gawlgeen' be /gɔ:l'gi:n/ or / 'gɔ:lgi:n /?

This lack of restriction on the placing of stress causes considerable difficulty to foreigners whose own language regularly places stress in the same position, as for example Swahili which places the stress on the penultimate syllable, so that ''jiko' / 'dʒi:ko / becomes ji'koni / dʒi:'ko:ni / when a prepositional suffix is added. In French too, the stress will normally always occur on the same, but here the final, syllable.

So far I have talked about word stress, i.e. where the stress is placed on isolated words. What is perhaps more important in English is rhythmic stress, which may obscure, or even conflict with normal word stress in a stream of speech. This will be dealt with later in the chapter.

INTONATION

Given a collection of words, say 'love', 'John' and 'Mary' and a structural pattern which arranges them as 'John loves Mary', you have meaning. But only, so far, part of the meaning. By adding other linguistic components to the words and the pattern we can add to the meaning, or rather complete it. Should these three words occur in conversation we are likely to obtain much more information than is conveyed by the written statement. We will, when listening to the speaker, most likely be able to ascertain that the speaker:

(a) thinks that this statement reports a fact; or
(b) is querying whether it is in fact *John* (or someone else) who loves Mary; or
(c) is querying whether John loves *Mary* (or someone else); or
(d) is querying whether John *loves* her (or merely likes her, or knows her); or
(e) is stating that it is *John,* (and not anyone else) who loves Mary; or

(*f*) is stating that it is *Mary*, (not Jane,) that John loves; or

(*g*) is stating that John *loves* Mary (doesn't hate her, or merely like her).

In addition we may also find out that the speaker:

(*h*) disapproves of the whole business; or

(*i*) is delighted with the news; or

(*j*) is bored with the news; or

(*k*) is sceptical of the news,

and so on. Other interpretations are possible.

In the case of (*a*)–(*g*) the interpretation is based on 'rules' of the English language which are as consistent and forceful as the 'rules' which say that 'love' means one thing and 'hate' another, or that 'I' is followed by 'am' rather than 'is'. They are as much linguistic rules as the so-called 'rules' of grammar. The fact that these 'tune rules' have not yet been fully codified or described does not invalidate this statement, since it has been realised that in many ways there is no complete description of any modern English 'rules', whether of grammar or **intonation**. In spite of the shelves full of English 'grammars', many of them admirably full and compendious, others sketchy and inaccurate or based on false premises, a complete description of English is still awaited. The study of English intonation is still incomplete, but at least its crucial importance as a factor needing to be taught to foreigners as much as grammar and vocabulary is being realised, and those 'rules' which give us (*a*)–(*g*) above can indeed be described with a fair degree of accuracy.

Similar rules will have to be applied to give the interpretations suggested in (*h*)–(*k*) and other utterances like these, but here the interpretation by the hearer is likely to rely on other features as well. These other features may well include gesture, facial expression and other voice features which are sometimes called **paralinguistic**. These features include such things as the quality of the voice—creaky, husky, whispery, falsetto, and so on, or even the accompaniment of other non-speech sounds such as giggles, laughter, sobs or snorts. These other factors are not yet susceptible of measurement or objective judgement,

49

although no native speaker has difficulty in knowing how to use or interpret them. Some work is being done on the measurement of such features.

As far as (a)–(g) are concerned, it will be seen that the varying interpretations placed on 'John loves Mary', were variations of fact. With (h)–(k) the variations were of the attitude of the speaker towards the fact. Written language, by means of punctuation and devices such as italicising, can often indicate the variations of factual meaning, but the attitudinal variations will normally only be apparent from context, or by the addition of some such comments as '. . . said Philip with a laugh', or '. . . she said incredulously'. The way in which these variations are effected in speech, is by means of voice 'tunes', i.e. by the pitch of the voice rising and falling in particular ways. Any English utterance pronounced in a monotone sounds unnatural, and monotone will rarely be used except perhaps on stage or in church for some particular effect. Even the shortest and simplest utterance will be said with some degree of pitch rise and fall; the place and amount of rise and fall will give that extra amount of information lacking in the written 'John loves Mary'. Any one 'tune' will run over a certain limited stretch of speech, sometimes corresponding to a sentence, more often not. For instance, 'Is he coming today?' will probably have one tune, here corresponding to the sentence, but 'If you don't mind, I'll come tomorrow' will usually have two tunes in the one sentence. The number of tunes in any one utterance will obviously bear some relation to the length of the utterance, but will not correlate wholly. Thus in 'Yes if you like' there may be either one tune (probably indicating a rather off-hand agreement), or two (probably indicating doubt as to the wisdom of your liking whatever it is). Any one tune is called an **intonation group.**

In each intonation group there will be one syllable which, as it were, takes the 'brunt' of the tune. On this syllable, which is stressed, the main change of pitch, rising, falling, rising and falling, falling and rising, is heard, though other syllables near it may lead up to or away from the main pitch direction. This syllable is called the **tonic**, or **nucleus**. By varying the choice of tonic syllable within the intonation group, *the meaning* of the group is changed. For instance, in 'John went fishing yesterday', if 'John' is selected as the tonic, the meaning is that John, not Bill went. If 'yesterday' is selected as tonic, the meaning becomes that he went yesterday, not today. If 'fishing' is tonic, it indicates that fishing was the activity rather than swimming, or something else. This choice of a particular syllable corresponds, of course, to what has customarily been described as 'emphasising' a particular word, and we can, by various devices such as prolonging the vowel in the syllable, saying it more loudly, and so on, vary the degree of emphasis we want to attach to a particular word or syllable. In the majority of utterances, however, it is not so much a question of emphasis, as of indicating our meaning by choosing the location of the tonic syllable, just as we choose one word rather than another. If we say 'I like this hat' instead of 'I hate this hat', we are indicating by choice of word what we mean. If we say 'I like this hat' with the tonic on 'this' instead of on 'like' we are again simply indicating our meaning. It is not so much a question of intonation emphasising an idea, but of intonation being used to convey meaning. This means that intonation is an integral part of the way in which we convey meaning, not something additional, superimposed on meaning, a 'frill' as it were. For this reason anyone learning English as a foreign language must be taught the basic rules of English intonation with as much care as he is taught the grammatical structures or the vocabulary. (Such things will, of course, normally be taught in the form of oral practice rather than as lists of rules.)

Let us look at some of the basic tunes of English. This can only be a rather sketchy outline, and it is suggested that readers interested in this aspect should study a text such as *The Intonation of Colloquial English* by J. D. O'Connor and G. F. Arnold, which, although primarily devised for foreign learners, will be illuminating to native English speakers unaccustomed to realising how much they rely on this means of communication.

One misconception should perhaps be cleared away first of all. It is the misleading and incomplete statement often made that falling intonations mark statements and rising ones questions.

It might be easier if English intonation had as simple a basic pattern as this, but unfortunately it is not true, as will be seen. It is however true to say that a falling tune tends to sound definite and complete, indicating that the speaker is treating what he says as a self-contained, separate item of interest. This applies to low falling, high falling and rise-falling tones (see below). With a rising tune it is less easy to generalise; some low rising tunes invite a response and are therefore incomplete sounding, others sound reassuring. The high-rising tune on the other hand nearly always tends to suggest a question in many European languages. The fall-rising tune has many uses about which it is difficult to generalise. Combinations of these various tunes are furthermore possible, so that the number of tunes available to express attitudes is very large and so is the degree of subtlety of attitude which can be expressed by intonation.

The basic tunes are therefore:

(*a*) The low fall. Here the voice on the tonic syllable starts at an already low pitch, but during the syllable falls to a slightly lower pitch. This is indicated by this mark before the appropriate syllable: ‚cheese.

(*b*) The high fall. Here the voice is at a fairly high pitch, but then falls to a lower pitch. Indicated by this mark: `cheese.

(*c*) The rise-fall. Here the voice starts on a mid pitch, rises slightly and then falls again. This is indicated as: ^cheese.

(*d*) The low rise. Voice starts on a low pitch and rises slightly. Indicated by: ‚cheese.

(*e*) The high rise. Voice starts at a mid or high pitch and rises even higher. Indicated thus: ′cheese.

(*f*) The fall-rise. Voice first falls and then rises to a mid or fairly high pitch. Thus: ˇcheese.

While a full analysis of the uses of these tunes is not here possible, we can see some of the great variety which is possible even within the use of one tune, by looking at some of the ways in which one of them, the low fall, is used.

If the low fall is used in statements, the general attitude conveyed is an unemotional one, rather neutral, or possibly even dull or surly. Examples are given in the right-hand column below. The left-hand column gives the conversational context:

1. What's your favourite game? ˌChess.
2. Do you like sugar in your tea? ˌNo.
3. Can you help me again please? ˌLater.

If the statement is longer, there will be a number of syllables from which it will be necessary to select one to carry the main pitch change.

4. Who left this money lying here? ˌMary did I think.
5. Why did you miss the train? Because I overˌslept.
6. Who said you couldn't come? ˌMother said so.

The same low fall tune can be used in asking questions, but again the attitude of the speaker is rather detached and aloof and sometimes even hostile.

7. You can tell where it came from. ˌHow can you tell?
8. I'm going to see Mary. ˌWhen are you going?
9. It's a good book. ˌWhich book do you mean?

When the low fall is used for commands, a calm, controlled attitude is indicated.

10. Can I have an orange? Take ˌtwo if you like.
11. What shall I do with the shopping? Put it down ˌthere.

Sometimes the low fall is used to convey sarcasm. A beautiful example is found in the popular song 'There's a Hole in my Bucket' in the Belafonte recording[1] with the following sequence:

12. With what shall I wet it? Try ˌwater, dear Henry.

This recording is well worth studying for the use of English intonation patterns, on which ninety per cent of the humour relies.

1. R.C.A. 1247. Harry Belafonte and Odetta, *There's a Hole in My Bucket.*

53

Finally, the low fall can be used for interjections, which will then usually sound unsurprised, and again calm and detached.

13. Do you take sugar?   ˌThank you.
14. He's coming to drinks tonight.   ˌGood.
15. I've won a prize.   Lucky ˌyou.

These examples have mainly illustrated variations of attitudes, but it is important to remember that the choice of tonic syllable, plus choice of tune, can make fairly radical differences of meaning. Look at the following:

16. I can't make ˌbread.   Low fall on 'bread'.
   (Statement finished, neutral.)
17. I can't make ˇbread.   Fall rise on 'bread'.
   (*Implication:* but I can make cakes.)
18. ˈI can't make bread.   High fall on 'I'.
   (*Implication:* but you can.)
19. ˇI can't make bread.   Fall rise on 'I'.
   (*Implication:* are you joking?)
20. I can't ˌmake bread.   Low fall on 'make'.
   (*Implication:* but I can buy it.)

As has been said, the basis of the tune is the selection of the tonic syllable, and the selection of the appropriate pitch change centred on that syllable. But in a longer intonation group, other syllables than the tonic will have some degree of stress, and the number of stressed syllables, and the pitch on which they are pronounced relative to the pitch of the tonic syllable will vary according to the intentions of the speaker, and give the speaker much scope for further varying the subtlety of the attitude he wishes to indicate. Stressed syllables coming before the tonic syllable are usually referred to as occurring in the head or pre-head, and syllables coming after the tonic syllable constitute the tail.

RHYTHMIC STRESS

It is necessary to make the distinction between word stress, discussed above, and **rhythmic stress**. While any word pronounced in isolation will have a stress, or stresses on particular syllables, it is not true that in normal running speech any word will necessarily have a stress at all. For example:

21. (a) 'going.   Word stress on first syllable   'going.

(b) I'm 'going whether you like it or not.   Tonic syllable 'go', stress as on word in isolation.

(c) I'm not going to 'tell you.   No stress at all on 'go', since tonic is now on 'tell'.

22. (a) 'over. Word stress on first syllable   'o.
(b) 'Over you go   Tonic syllable 'o, stress as on word in isolation.

(c) It's over an 'hour since he came.   No stress on 'o', since tonic now on 'hour'.

The tendency in English is to select nouns, verbs, adverbs, adjectives and pronouns for stressing, according to the degree of importance we wish to attach to them, but there is no invariable rule either that these parts of speech should be stressed, or that other parts may not be stressed. One of the principal characteristics of English speech, however, is the presence of rhythmic stress. This means, briefly, that English speakers have a tendency to stress syllables at roughly equal spaces in time, so that the decision as to which syllables are to be stressed will depend partly on meaning and partly on timing. One result is that if the meaning seems to demand two stressed syllables in close proximity, they will tend to be spaced out by being made more slowly and deliberately, whereas if a lot of 'unimportant' syllables occur between two on which stress is felt to be necessary, they will tend to be spoken rapidly. Compare:

23. In a couple of 'minutes dear . . .
24. 'Ten 'minutes only . . .

Here the four syllables in 'in a couple of . . .' will probably take only as much time to say as 'ten'.

It may take a little practice to pick out the stressed syllables in the longer intonation groups, but it is not really difficult. It is easy and obvious in some poetry and much doggerel:

25. '*Humpty*'*Dumpty*'*sat on a*'*wall,*
    '*Humpty*'*Dumpty*'*had a great*'*fall.*
26. *The* '*Assyrians came* '*down like a* '*wolf on the* '*fold*
    Their '*cohorts were* '*gleaming with* '*purple and* '*gold.*

The rhythms of ordinary speech are more subtle and less thumping, but clearly exist. The foreigner who does not master them will always sound a foreigner, however impeccable in theory his vowels and consonants; this applies particularly to the foreigner who insists on stressing what are normally unstressed 'weak' syllables since the fact that they are stressed distorts the actual vowel quality, as will be shown in the next section.

CONNECTED SPEECH

Considerable confusion is often caused to beginners in phonetic studies by the fact that the pronunciation of words in English can be quite different when they are said in isolation and when they occur in the ordinary run of speech. The classic example is perhaps 'the', usually pronounced 'thee' / ði: / if it is talked about or quoted, but never pronounced so in ordinary conversation, where it will usually be / ðə /, or before a vowel / ði / (short), or even just / ð /.

This fact can be explained by an analysis of the effect of stressing on vowel quantity and quality, but there are also other factors which affect the pronunciation of any one word or syllable in connected speech.

Let us take a short passage and write it out firstly in ordinary writing which can be taken to represent fairly rapid colloquial speech, then in a broad phonemic transcription and finally, as a series of isolated words:

(i)   One more place he walked to next day was Westminster

Abbey. Then he went to a good concert before catching the night train to Scotland.

(ii)   wəm mɔː pleis i wɔːk tə neks dei wəz wesminstə æbi. ðen i wen tə ə gug kɔnsət bifɔː kætʃiŋ ðə nai trein tə skɔ ʔlən.

(iii)	wɔn	tu	æbiː	went	kɔnsət	nait
	mɔː	nekst	ðen	tu	biːfɔː	trein
	pleis	dei	hiː	ei	kætʃiŋ	tu
	hiː	wɔz				
	wɔːkt	westminstə		gud	ðiː	skɔtlənd.

The main differences in pronunciation between isolated words and words in connected speech can be analysed under the following headings, and examples of each can be found by comparing (ii) and (iii) above.

(*a*)   The dropping of initial / h / in words like 'he' or 'him' is usual in colloquial speech unless the word occurs at the beginning of a sentence or after a pause, or unless it is stressed for a particular reason. In the passage above therefore / hiː / becomes / i / in the connected version.

(*b*)   Vowel quality and quantity tend to change according to whether the syllable is stressed or unstressed in connected speech. Thus / wɔn / becomes / wən / in connected speech if not stressed, and / wɔz/ becomes / wəz /, / tu / becomes / tə /.

(*c*)   Consonantal sounds at the end of a word are often influenced by the following consonant. Thus / gud / becomes / gug / under the influence of the following velar consonant. Similarly / wɔn / may become / wəm / before a following / m /. This is known as assimilation. It does not necessarily always occur, but may do so, and with some speakers is habitual.

(*d*)   The difference between careful and ordinary colloquial pronunciation may sometimes be seen in the loss of a sound (elision). Examples here are / nekst / becoming / neks / or / wɔːkt / becoming / wɔːk /. Only a very careful speaker would probably insert the / t / sound in the first syllable of 'Westminster', although many people believe that they do.

(*e*)   Very few people will pronounce the two alveolar plosives

c   57 in 'Scotland' except in very careful, isolated pronunciation. The first will usually be replaced by a glottal stop and the second will either vanish or be unexploded.

Many of the features occurring in rapidly spoken forms have traditionally come under the general accusation of being 'sloppy' or 'incorrect' or even 'uneducated'. It is important to realise that these accusations are, for the most part, quite unfounded and that everyone, including the most educated and respected speakers, is likely to use these alternative forms quite naturally and correctly. In fact to use other allegedly more 'correct' forms would result in completely foreign or stilted speech. Try saying rapidly:

(iv) wɔn mɔː pleis hiː wɔːkt tu nekst dei wɔz Westminstə æbiː ...

and you will soon see how difficult it is, and how unnatural, even if the effort succeeds. The question of 'correctness' is, however, taken up in more detail later in the book. One further point which may be made here, however, is that if the passage at (i) is read aloud (as it is almost bound to be by readers of this book) the pronunciation will vary between the version given at (ii) and the more stilted version of (iv). The version at (ii) is based on ordinary colloquial rapid speech. Reading is inevitably less 'natural', and probably less rapid and will therefore not be a reflection of normal speech habits. Where possible tape recordings of unrehearsed conversation (preferably where the participants are not aware of the presence of the recorder!) will best illustrate the veracity of the points made about colloquial speech.

5
The Patterns of Language

In the last chapter it was pointed out that quite a sensible, if limited conversation could be carried out by intonation only, tunes without words. It is also true that a considerable amount of information can be conveyed from one speaker, or writer, to another person, without the use of intonation, and with the use of only a minimal number of known or recognised words, the rest of the words being either unknown or nonsensical. The fewer there are of any such words in an utterance, the easier of course it is to 'guess' the meaning, but it is possible to eliminate a very considerable number of known words, and still retain some potential meanings. For example:

		Unknowns
(a)	The boy hooked an eight-pound samaki in the river.	(one)
(b)	The grint book is on the froom.	(two)
(c)	Plat clothes are fashionable among the tanging youth in Lodlickee.	(three)
(d)	The grinting bidoms are juzzling in the temach today.	(four)
(e)	The siffling, linsome witters will fazacle you if you nek them allerly.	(six)

And so on.

What in fact does the 'guessing' consist of? Teachers will frequently urge pupils to 'guess' at the meaning of words they have not met before. 'Guessing', in this sort of instance, is in fact a process superficially intuitive, but in reality based on two main analytical processes which the student performs. The first type of analysis is based on deduction from context. The hearer examines various possible concepts for the unknown word, eliminating some and reserving others as possible, according

59

to whether or not such concepts relate intelligibly to the other concepts in the utterance. Thus in (*a*) above, the context makes it clear that a 'samaki' is something that can be hooked, that can weigh eight pounds, and that is found in a river. On these grounds, items such as 'car', 'house', 'desk' or 'elephant' would be rejected, but items such as 'salmon', 'fish', 'perch' might be retained. The second analysis that student 'guessing' consists of would reject words such as 'fishy', 'heavy', 'edible', 'smelly', and so on, as meanings for 'samaki', not because there is any incompatibility between these concepts and the other concepts in the sentence, but because there is incompatibility between the forms of these words and the setting, 'an eight-pound . . . in the river. 'Guessing' therefore eliminates these forms. If it is possible to eliminate all potential replacements for 'samaki' on the ground of (*a*) incompatibility of context, and (*b*) incompatibility of form, the students will be left with a rather restricted range of possible 'meanings' for the unknown word, and the only true 'guess-work' then consists of selecting from this range.

This chapter is largely concerned with the second type of analysis, which is one that we all tend to perform constantly and unconsciously, and which in fact is instrumental in allowing us to understand a very considerable amount of what is said to us, or what we read.

(*b*) 'The grint book is on the froom.' We have little difficulty here in deciding that 'grint' is an adjective and 'froom' a noun, though many of us may find it rather difficult to say why. Our mastery of the patterns of our language is nearly complete quite early in childhood, and if we never have reason to analyse them, it is often difficult to explain our knowledge. Most of us are taught enough schoolroom grammar to cope with terms such as 'noun', 'adjective' and 'verb' with a greater or lesser degree of assurance, but in most cases our theory and practice are very divergent. Our theory may tell us that a noun is a name of a place, person or thing, but this will not account for the fact that we judge 'froom' in our sentence to be a noun, since we can have no acquaintanceship with whatever it is supposed to be a name of. And how do we know that 'grint' describes a 'book', since this is the reason we are most likely to give for saying that 'grint' is an adjective? In fact our carefully learnt theory is here useless, but our native experience tells us rapidly and much more reliably that 'froom' must be a noun because it comes after 'in the . . .' and we have no experience of any single word following these two that is not what we have learnt to call a 'noun'. Similarly experience tells us that between 'the' and 'book' we are most likely to have an adjective, or else possibly a 'noun used as an adjective' (e.g. 'The China question is important'), and therefore that 'grint' must be an adjective.

Native experience, then, gives us a mastery over a whole series of complicated patterns of which we are largely unaware. 'Sequence of tenses' is a difficult exercise in Latin, or for foreigners learning English, but even less well educated native speakers will say 'I'd've done it earlier if only I'd thought', without difficulty, and without need of being taught rules about pluperfects, conditionals, and so on. It is the job of the linguist consciously to explore and describe the patterns, finding regular shapes in even the most apparently free-ranging, spontaneous and original utterances. Statistical degrees of probability can, at least theoretically, be established for anything we say; as Miller says, 'It is a bit surprising to find that one's verbal behaviour follows such statistical rules with considerable orderliness. We select our words and arrange them to communicate with others with no consideration for relative frequencies of occurrence. Still, on the average, this apparently wilful and conscious behaviour of choosing words follows statistical rules with great regularity. Like the man who suddenly discovered he had been writing prose all his life, most of us find it rather wonderful that we can behave so lawfully with no trouble at all.'[1]

What are these patterns? What are they made up of? If a knitting pattern is based on the stitch, what are language patterns based on? What are the basic units of language? The answer to this is by no means simple and will tend to vary according to the use to which we want to put the answer. What may at first sight appear the obvious answer to the layman—

1. George A. Miller, *Language and Communication*. McGraw-Hill.

the word—is often a good answer, but sometimes it may be preferable to say the 'sentence', or the 'morpheme', or even the 'phoneme'. Language, in fact, is built up of a whole series of patterns, each type of unit having a pattern of its own and each interlocking and interacting with other patterns at other levels.

Since 'linguistics' in its modern sense is a relatively new science, still largely exploratory and tentative, there is no universal agreement on how to describe the patterns of language, or even on what the patterns consist of. As in many other areas of language, the way in which we decide to describe, is to some extent determined by the purpose of the description. The rest of this chapter is no exception. Much of it is loosely based on descriptions which follow a theory of grammar called 'scale and category', formulated by Professor Michael Halliday (see Chapter 8), but, where necessary, these descriptions are adapted, extended or simplified to suit the present purpose, which is to try to show the non-linguist some of the intricacies of patterning in his own or any other language, and the complexity of structure in even the simplest utterance.

Let us say, then, that the grammatical patterns of language are made up of five different types of unit, **morpheme, word, group, clause** and **sentence**, each with its own structure. In examining each of these units and analysing its own internal structure, it will be seen that the units adjacent to it are also thereby being described, so that a complex interrelationship is gradually built up.

MORPHEME

'House' and 'houses' are both words, as are 'talk' and 'talking'. You may say that the difference between the nouns 'house' and 'houses', or between the verbs 'talk' and 'talking' is grammatical, in that 'house' is followed by a singular verb, 'houses' by a plural verb, and that 'talk' as a verb can immediately follow a subject, while 'talking' as part of a verbal group has to have an auxiliary between it and a subject; or you may choose to say that the meaning is different—'houses' meaning 'more than one house', 'talking' implying an activity in course of progression, while the time or aspect is less definite in 'talk'. Either explanation hinges on the fact that something is added in the second form. 'Houses', in our terms, consists of two morphemes, 'house' and 's', each of which has a grammatical function. We cannot take any other part of the word, separate it off, and say that the detached part makes a distinctive contribution to the 'grammar' of the word, e.g. we cannot say that 'h' adds a meaning or a function to 'ouse' (although it may add social status to the speaker!), or that 't' adds grammatically to 'alk'—neither 't' nor 'alk' have any independent meaningful existence. A morpheme then is a minimal grammatical form. Neither length, nor syllable, is any guide to identifying the morphemes in a stretch of language. Thus 'I', 'honeymoon' and 'Timbuktu' are equally single morphemes. The fact that 'honey' and 'moon' can, in other circumstances, have independent morpheme status does not mean that, nowadays, in 'honeymoon' they have such independent status. On the other hand, short words like 'cats', 'oxen' and 'comes' are all two-morpheme words. Words like 'his' and 'were' cause some controversy, some linguists preferring to treat them as single, others as two morpheme 'fused' words, so that 'were' can be regarded as 'is' + (past) = 'were', and 'his' as 'he' + (possession) = 'his'. With words like 'sheep' where singular and plural forms are identical, some linguists like to say that 'sheep' (plural) = sheep + (plural), with the rider that (plural) here = zero, but these and other refinements need not here be gone into. Although there is room for much argument on morpheme status, the general principle is a clear and useful one when studying the patterns of language. A morpheme, then, cannot be further broken up into grammatical parts, though it can, of course, on a different level, be broken up into phonemes which, when assembled, give it its distinctive meaning.

A useful distinction is that between a 'free' and a 'bound' morpheme. If a single morpheme stands alone and constitutes a word, (e.g. 'I', 'walk', 'song', 'rubbish'), it is said to be **free**. If it can be used only in association with at least one other morpheme (e.g. 'ed' in 'walked', 'ster' in 'songster', 's' in 'roses'), it is **bound**. Another, more familiar, way of looking at

63

morphemes is in the traditional classification into **roots** and **affixes** (suffixes and prefixes). A bound morpheme will be a suffix or prefix in English (though there are other forms of affix in some other languages). A root will more often be free, but can be bound (e.g. '-ceive' in 'receive', 'deceive', 'conceive'), and the great majority of English morphemes are in fact free, and roots. Some forms can of course be either; for instance, 'post' can be a bound morpheme as in '*post*pone', or a similar form can be a free morpheme as in 'the *post* goes at four o'clock'. Two separate morphemes are here involved. Almost any root can have affixes added, and even if the resulting word is a 'new' one, i.e. if there is no evidence of its having appeared before in speech or writing, the native English speaker will be able to deduce its meaning quite safely by basing his interpretation on his knowledge of the morphemic structure of English words. For example:

pig:	free morpheme, root.
pigly:	free morpheme + bound morpheme -ly.
piglily:	free morpheme + 2 bound morphemes -li and -ly.
pigliness:	free morpheme + 2 bound morphemes -li and -ness.

Although the chances are that the reader will not have met the last three forms, he will have little difficulty in analysing them morphemically and in recognising the differences conveyed by the bound morphemes, whether he chooses to state the difference grammatically, ('-ly' makes it into an adjective or an adverb), or in terms of meaning ('-ly' means 'like a pig'). Conversely, confronted by *'lypig'[1] or *'linesspig' he will be at a loss; the constituents 'ly' 'pig' and 'ness' are still there, but because the patterning is not recognisable as an English pattern, meaning is lost. Meaning does not therefore derive solely from the individual morphemes, but also from their patterning, or arrangement, which is normally fairly simple, but can become very complex, as in the favourite 'antidisestablishmentarianism',

1. As elsewhere in the text, a form preceded by an asterisk indicates its non-existence in the language.

where even minor disruption of patterning leads to gibberish.

The morphemic structure of English words gives considerable opportunity for poetic invention, an opportunity which many modern poets have seized. Considerable subtlety of meaning can also be conveyed by appropriate choice of bound morpheme, since certain affixes have acquired rather different meanings. Think for example of '-y', '-ish' and '-ing' and the effect they have when added to say, 'yellow'. Though it is difficult perhaps on a factual basis to distinguish between 'yellowish', 'yellowy' and 'yellowing' most English people would use each of them rather differently, but this is a point which will be further taken up in Chapter 6. e e cummings used elements which we think of as bound morphemes, as free morphemes in some of his poetry:

1. *a dapper derbied*
   creature, swaggers daintily
   twiddling
   his tiny cane
   and mazurkas about tweak-
   ing his wing collar pecking at his im-
   peccable cravat directing being
   shooting his cuffs
   saluted everywhere saluting
   reviewing processions of minions
   tappingpeopleontheback . . .[1]

where the distinction between word and morpheme becomes blurred, for are we to regard 'im' as an independent word, or as bound morpheme? Similarly, in the last line, the distinction between word and group is blurred.

Dylan Thomas, Hopkins and other poets have used this property of English to coin new combinations, often with dramatic or refreshing effect. One example may perhaps be given:

2.   *It was my thirtieth year to heaven*
     Woke to my hearing from harbour and neighbour wood

1. e e cummings 'Two X' in *Faber Book of Modern Verse*.

65

> *And the mussel pooled and the heron*
> *priested shore*
> *The morning beckon*
> *With water praying and call of seagull and rook*
> *And the knock of sailing boats on the net webbed wall*
> *Myself to set foot*
> *That second*
> *In the still sleeping town and set forth.*[1]

'Mussel pooled' and 'heron priested' may be unorthodox, but present no real difficulty to anyone with native intuitive mastery of English morphemic patterning.

WORD

In discussing the morpheme, I have inevitably and frequently talked about the word, without specifying what in fact is mean, by a word. That it should need specifying may seem surprising, but the task of definition is not so easy as one might imagine. Consider the following (and the e e cummings poem on p. 65).

3. 'One gets very confused all over the isms and ologies today.'
4. 'It's abso-blooming-lutely luverly'[2]
5. 'Pimpernelseek for the tiptop computerman who can take the firm to Bits and put them together again making too-too the en beansfive.'[3]

Asked to list the 'words' in 1, 3, 4, and 5, there may be hesitation over certain items, but by and large, we are likely to take our cue from the typographer who had to decide how to set the type, and we will decide that anything with a space on either side is probably a word. We might then say that a word is anything which can be written with a space on either side of it, and we may thus have a useful working guide, but in fact we have merely shunted the responsibility back on to the writer

1. Dylan Thomas 'Poem in October'.
2. Quoted in B. Strang 'Modern English Structure', from *The Times*, August 1960.
3. Quoted in *The Professional Engineer*, Vol. 11, No. 4, November 1966. Part of an advertisement in 'Situations Vacant' in August 1966.

or typographer. The fact remains had we had to make the decision, it is likely we would have agreed with the typographer and that there is likely to be something near unanimity in such decisions. For practical purposes therefore, the 'definition' is a workable one, that a word is anything which can be written with a space on either side of it.

Bloomfield, one of the fathers of modern linguistics, gave what has become one of the classic modern definitions of a word in the following paragraph:

> A free form which consists entirely of two or more lesser free forms, as for instance 'poor John' or 'John ran away' or 'yes, sir,' is a *phrase*. A free form which is not a phrase, is a *word*. A word then, is a free form which does not consist entirely of (two or more) lesser free forms; in brief, a word is a *mimimum free form*.[1]

In considering speech as opposed to writing, however, there are difficulties with this definition. There is no doubt that 'I' is in some sense a minimum free form, and is always written between spaces. In French 'je', 'y' and 'en' are written between spaces, but can these act as minimum free forms in speech? It is difficult, in English, to contrive a conversation where 'I' will stand alone, though in reading aloud or reciting one may say, ' "I," said the sparrow, "with my little arrow, I shot Cock Robin",' or in grammatical discussions about the item, one may use it alone: ' "Is I or me correct in 'It's $\left. \begin{matrix} \text{I} \\ \text{me} \end{matrix} \right\}$ he told to go'?" "I".' But these examples are insufficient evidence of the general acceptability of 'I' as a minimum free form in speech. And what Frenchman would ever say 'je' or 'y' or 'en' on their own?

On the other hand, utterances such as / ŋkju: / = written 'Thank you', or / dzedu: / = written 'how do you do?' are barely separable into independent word constituents, though perfectly normal, acceptable forms of educated speech.

These are some of the difficulties of ascertaining what a (spoken) word is, and it may seem unfair that no solution should be offered. The reason is that there is no simple solution,

1. Bloomfield, *Language*, George Allen & Unwin.

and as in so many areas of linguistics, difficulties are opened up which in themselves are illuminating, but which need much more thought and research before (if ever) definitive solutions can be offered. The identity of the spoken word is better for the moment taken to be the same as that of the written word, unsatisfactory as this is from many points of view. Most of us have been brought up to believe that the written and spoken word are the same, and although our ears may constantly contradict us, we have for the moment no other workable assumption. To sum up then, a word is not perhaps so easily defined as it might appear, but for working purposes, it is that stretch of language which can be written between spaces. We can also say that a word is composed of one or more than one morpheme, and that the morphemic patterning in an English word to some extent determines its meaning.

Before passing on to the patterning of combinations of words, it is necessary to make a distinction between two different types of words: those sometimes called **lexical** and **grammatical** (or **structural**) words. As a very rough and ready guide, grammatical words will be those you can with reasonable safety omit in a telegram, lexical words are those which you will have to include. In composing your telegram there may also be words about which you hesitate—will their exclusion lead to ambiguity; is their inclusion strictly necessary? These words probably have some of the properties of both lexical and grammatical words. Lexical words belong to an **open set**—it is virtually impossible to list them exhaustively, and it is always possible to replace them by others, and to make new ones. They will usually be nouns, verbs, adjectives or adverbs. Grammatical words on the other hand belong to **closed systems**, the members of which can be completely listed. Their numbers will only rarely be added to, or altered. There are times, however, when it is difficult to assign one or other property to a particular word. An example might be the word 'request' as used in a telegraphic context, e.g. in 'Delegation arriving tomorrow request send transport'. 'Request' is here part of a closed set of words (others are 'please' and 'grateful') which might be omitted with safety, if discourtesy. In other contexts of course, 'request'

68

might be a fully lexical word. Prepositions also tend to occupy an intermediate status between fully grammatical and fully lexical words.

FORM AND MEANING

At this point it is perhaps worth breaking off to repeat more formally what was assumed in the early part of the chapter and what must have become more obvious later on. In the traditional grammar on which most of us were brought up, the chief disadvantage of which is that while it fits Latin it doesn't always fit English, definition of 'parts of speech' and grammatical analysis generally depended almost wholly, at least in theory, on taking meaning as a standard of judgement by which definitions were made. Because this tended to lead sometimes to anomalies and confusion, some linguists, particularly in America, attempted to formulate a grammar which would not rely on meaning for its definitions and analysis, but on form, i.e. the technical arrangement and structure of the language. In fact of course, traditional grammar often did this too, even if not overtly, so that most people decided that 'travel' in 'Travel broadens the mind' was a noun, and 'travel' in 'I travel to broaden my mind' was a verb, on the basis of their respective positions in the sentence, rather than on any application of the doctrines about 'naming' words and 'doing' words. Early attempts at excluding meaning from grammar were either misunderstood, or in their turn found lacking, and more recently there has been greater recognition that 'native intuition' (i.e. reference to what the speaker or hearer understands the meaning to be) has to be taken into account in any grammatical statement. (See Chapter 8.)

Nevertheless, a study of language which is based primarily on form, or structure, is likely to be more fruitful for most purposes for which grammatical descriptions are used, including the teaching of languages. The fact that any such grammatical description will more often than not come to similar conclusions to those reached by traditional grammar is not surprising, but the different reasons for coming to those conclusions must be recognised. Thus, even if books on language continue to refer to 'noun' and 'verb' and use other terms familiar from school grammar, this is purely for convenience and does not necessarily imply a traditional definition of them.

One of the main difficulties for anyone coming fresh to the study of linguistics, is in fact this question of terminology. At this stage of development of the science, each linguist tends to use terms in his own way and readers must be warned that one man's morpheme is another man's poison, that A's clause is B's sentence and that each linguist will probably have at least one or two terms unique to him- or herself which can only be understood by careful reference to that particular author's own definition (or implication, for in common with many scientists, linguists nowadays are often chary of definition in itself).

GROUP

Nominal Group
Consider the following:

    (*a*) John saw Mary.
    (*b*) The man had built a house.
    (*c*) The old man had been writing some letters.
    (*d*) The man who came to dinner is thought to have stolen a wallet full of notes.

Let us suppose that 'the man' in (*b*), 'the old man' in (*c*), and 'the man who came to dinner' in (*d*) were all called John. Each of the sentences could quite well be rewritten, stating 'John had built . . .' 'John had been writing . . .' or 'John is thought to have . . .' The single word 'John' in these rewritten sentences stands for a group of two words in (*b*), three in (*c*), and six in (*d*). Each of these groups of words forms the subject of the sentence. Any group of words found at subject position[1] in a sentence forms a **nominal group**. Nominal groups are also found elsewhere, for example as complements,[1] so that 'Mary'

---

1. 'Subject' and 'complement' can be formally defined but to do so here would be too involved and lengthy. Roughly, 'subject' = that part of the sentence which determines the form of the verb, 'complement' = the non-verbal part of the predicate.

in (*a*), 'a house' in (*b*), 'some letters' in (*c*) and 'a wallet full of notes' in (*d*) are all also nominal groups. Other places for nominal groups will be found, but these can for the moment be ignored. Discussion of how groups are used will form part of the discussion of sentence structuring (pp. 77 ff.). First however, let us look at the structure and patterning of the nominal groups themselves.

	I	2	3	4
(*a*)			John	
(*b*)	the		man	
(*c*)	the	old	man	
(*d*)	the		man	who came to dinner

In each of these, the group has a readily recognisable **head**, set out here in column 3. The head of a nominal group is the one element in it that might be considered indispensable, but there are certain types of subject where the nominal group is a clause, where it will be difficult to identify a head. For example:

(*e*)   *That he should have thought so* surprises me.

Here the part in italics is what governs the verb, and is therefore the subject, and therefore a nominal group. We shall see later that clauses can operate, as here, at positions normally occupied by groups, or rather the nominal group can have a clause form. For convenience, 'nominal group' is abbreviated to **ngp**.

Apart from groups of type (*e*) and one or two others, therefore, nominal groups will have a head. This will usually be what we are accustomed to calling a noun or pronoun. In describing the ngp **h** will be used as the symbol for head. In (*a*) there is only h, in (*b*) there is one item before the head, in (*c*) two items before the head, and in (*d*) one item before and one item after the head. It is useful to call those parts of an ngp which come before the head **modifiers**—**m**—and those which come after it, **qualifiers**—**q**—. We can then describe the structure of (*b*) as m h , of (*c*) as m m h , and of (*d*) as m h q .

The possible structure of a typical nominal group is then:

71

(m)   h   (q)

the brackets indicating that the presence of (m) and (q) is optional.

There may be more than one m, e.g.

(*f*) The	well-dressed,	redhaired,	45 year old	famous	actress
m	m	m	m	m	h

but it is more difficult to find examples of more than one or two q items:

(*g*) The	man	in a blue coat	who came to dinner ...
m	h	q	q

(*h*) The	man	without a coat	I met yesterday	who used to live
m	h	q	q	in Africa ...
				q

By the time one gets to three qualifiers most people feel rather uncomfortable, and even two is slightly clumsy. Modern English writing, especially journalism of a particular kind, and advertising, gives many examples of multiple modifiers. Recent advertisements for instance have included:

(*i*) 'superb blended woollen gabardine raincoat', and even better:

(*j*) '... the smooth cool creamy minty chewy round slow velvety fresh clean solid buttery taste of Nuttall's Mintoes.'

It is, however, far rarer to find more than one or two quali-fiers.

If needed, it is quite possible to classify the various m components and label separately such things as deictics—**d**—(words like 'the'), ordinals—**o**—(words like 'first'), epithets—**e**—(such as 'red'), and so on, so that one can in fact say that the structure of an ngp such as 'the first red gate on the left' is d o e h q , and the structure of ngps generally is (d) (o) (e) h (q). This is said to be carrying the description of the ngp to a greater stage, of **delicacy**, but is not for the present necessary to our purposes where it is adequate to describe the typical structure of an ngp as (m) h (q). It will be noticed, however, that the structures of the typical m and the typical q are quite different. An m is often a single word, and is rarely very complicated, while the q component is rarely simple, and often has a complicated structure of its own. In the sentences (d) and (g) above, the q is a 'who . . .' clause, in (h) two of the qualifiers are similar, while one is a three word prepositional phrase 'without a coat'.

Sometimes the head itself can be more complicated than any in the examples so far given:

(k) The birds and the bees in the cicada trees . . .

or

(l) Man, woman and child (are alike . . .)

In these **coordination** (page 80) accounts for a double, or triple h.

Verbal Group

In sentences (a) to (d) above, there were a number of ngp acting as subjects or complements of the sentences. In addition there were the elements 'saw' in (a), 'had built' in (b), 'had been writing' in (c) and 'is thought to have stolen' in (d). Each of these constitutes a **verbal group** (**vgp**). In (a) there is a simple, single-word group, but with the others there are increasing degrees of complexity. A verbal group will normally consist of a combination of **full** verbs and **auxiliaries**. Full verbs are open set lexical words (or better, lexical items), and auxiliaries are grammatical (closed system) items. Auxiliaries can be defined as those 'whose forms are used together with the negative particle, or to put it a better way, which have paired positive and negative forms'.[1] Thus the negative of 'I like it' is 'I don't like it' not 'I liken't it', whereas the negative of 'I can come' is 'I can't come'. Thus 'like' is a full verb, 'can' an auxiliary. Auxiliaries are sometimes divided themselves into two categories—the **primary**—have, be and do, and the **secondary**, or **modal**—will, shall, can, may, must, ought, dare, need, and used (/ juːst /).

1. F. R. Palmer, *A Linguistic Study of the English Verb*, Longmans.

73

Combinations of primary and secondary auxiliaries and lexical items can build up extremely complex structures, subject to complex rules. Verbal groups could, however be classified under five main types;

Those where:

(i)   there is a lexical item only;
(ii) the lexical item ends in -ing;
(iii) ,,   ,,   ,,   ,,   ,, -ed, -t, or -en;
(iv) ,,   ,,   ,, is the infinitive form without 'to';
(v)   ,,   ,,   ,, is the infinitive form plus 'to'.

Examples of these types are:

(*a*) John *saw* Mary.
(*b*) The old man *had been writing* some long letters.
(*c*) The man *had built* a house.
(*d*) The baby *can walk* now.
(*e*) He *ought to walk*.

In addition, it is possible to get a complex structure where the first item is not a closed system item (i.e. an auxiliary), but a lexical item. For example in 'he keeps jumping up and down', 'keeps', (not here used in the same way as in 'he keeps chickens') must be considered as a lexical item and not as an extra auxiliary. Other lexical items can participate in similar structures, which can become very lengthy and complex, as in 'I asked him to help her to persuade her mother to come'. When a lexical verb is used as the first item of a complex vgp it is called a **catenative** verb.

The term **lexical item** has been used in preference to lexical word, in order to include such things as 'turn off' (the light), 'look up' (a reference), or 'put up with' (discomfort). These combinations of words must be considered as single lexical items, although they consist of more than one word. The particles 'off', 'up', 'across', etc., when used in this way, are an inherent part of the lexical verb and cannot be dealt with in terms of 'prepositions', 'adverbs' or any other of the traditional classifications. Such multi-word verbs can themselves be divided into different types, but in dealing with the vgp they must be

74

regarded as single lexical items. The identification of some lexical items may be controversial. It is possible to make a good case for saying that items such as 'take part' (in a game), or 'get rid of' (rubbish) are also single lexical items, although 'part' and 'rid' do not otherwise share the characteristics of the other particles.

It will be obvious that not all auxiliaries can enter into all the patterns of types (i)–(v). For instance, one cannot have *he ought walk, or *he might to walk. Certain auxiliaries are restricted to certain patterns.

The verbal groups that have so far been discussed are all **finite**, in other words, they are closely associated with, and are governed by, a subject. Other verb forms are, however, **non-finite**, that is, their form does not depend upon a subject, and they can enter into different types of structure and perform different functions. Examples might be: '*Coming* up the hill, I met Mary', or '*Lost* in Hyde Park on Monday . . .'

A full study of the patterns of the English verbal group is, however, neither appropriate nor possible here. Anyone wishing to examine the patterning in greater detail should look at, for instance, F. R. Palmer, *A Linguistic Study of the English Verb*. As elsewhere, much of the method, and detail of patterning is controversial and much is very complex. In any full statement, for instance, it will be necessary to account for the fact that any difference in meaning between 'he started reading' and 'he started to read' is slight, whereas the difference between the superficially similar formal patterns of 'he wanted to wash' and 'he wanted washing' is far from slight. It is probable that the transformational approach to grammar (Chapter 8) is the one that will be most helpful here.

Adverbial Group

So far, groups of words occurring as subject, complement or verb in any sentence have been discussed. There remain a number of other items which will have to be accounted for.

(*a*) John was walking slowly.
(*b*) I went to town yesterday.

There are recognisable ngps at subject position (S), 'John' and 'I', vgps in the verbal position (V), 'was walking' and 'went', but there are left 'slowly' and 'to town yesterday'. In each case it is clear that they are not complements, but adjuncts (A) performing the function traditionally called adverbial. These **adverbial groups** (**agp**) may be quite simple, as in 'slowly'; slightly more complicated as in 'to town', where the two words form a structure (preposition (p) + prepositional complement (c)) of their own, or very complex as in the italicised parts of the following:

(*c*) The man waited for his friend *until the clock struck six.*

(*d*) John kicked the ball *with all the force he was capable of mustering in view of his recent recovery from influenza.*

In both (*c*) and (*d*) the adverbial groups obviously have complex structures of their own, structures of a kind which will be discussed in the next section.

Research work is in progress on the structure of agps but little is available. It seems likely that classification may eventually be along the lines of recognition of (i) single adverbs (often but not always marked in English by -ly endings); (ii) complex preposition plus complement groups, where the complement itself will have a structure which may be that of an ngp (e.g. 'in the big red house' = agp = p + c.   c = ngp = mmmh); and (iii) adverbial clauses recognised by certain introductory closed system items such as 'if' 'when' 'because', etc.

At this stage of linguistic study lack of research findings need not be too serious; recognition of an agp is intuitively simple and agrees closely with the traditional definition of adverbial function. It is enough to realise that sooner or later it will be possible to describe any agp in terms of its formal characteristics instead of having to rely on the traditional description, based on meaning, of an adverb as 'a word used to express the attribute of an attribute; one that qualifies an adjective, verb or another adverb' in the words of *The Shorter Oxford Dictionary* and then having to extend this definition of an adverb to 'phrases' or 'clauses'.

CLAUSES AND SENTENCES

In talking about groups, I referred to the places where they are found, i.e. as subjects, verbs, complements, and so on. There is a strictly limited number of such places in any sentence; in fact any major sentence, however complicated and lengthy, can have only one S place (subject) one V place (verb) one or two C places (complement) and a limited, but larger number of A places (adjunct). Any structure which contains:

> S V (C) (A), or occasionally
> V (C) (A)

will be either a **clause** or a **sentence**. As before, the brackets indicate that these components are optional, i.e. a clause or sentence may or may not contain complements or adjuncts. The following two examples are of (i) a very simple structure containing S V C A; and (ii) a much more complicated one which is nevertheless still basically only an S V C A structure.

(i) Mary	ate	her food	greedily
S	V	C	A

(ii) Girls who are greedy	like to eat	as much food as they can
S	V	C ...

get hold of	whenever they can do so without being seen
... C	A

The order of appearance of the S V C A components can be varied so that one may get, for instance A S V A or C S V, and so on, but any clause or major sentence can be described in terms of some arrangement of these four components. Look at some further examples.

(iii) The money	you	must give	me or Mary	(I don't care about the other things)
C	S	V	C	

(iv) As quickly as he could	he	ran	along the towpath.
A	S	V	A

77

(v) When the bell rang, | the girls who had passed the
          A   S ...

examinations | were reading | books which they had
    ... S   V   C ...

chosen the previous day |
     ... C

(vi) The dark man and the shorter, rather fat woman |
                      S

seem to be winning | the match
        V   C

(vii) I | gave | John | a blue suitcase and a valise full of clothes
     S| V | C   C

(viii) The crowd | pushed and surged and rocked | the gates
            S   V   C

You will notice that at S or C or A, the nominal or adverbial group may have a structure which itself contains an S V (C) (A) structure. This is, for the purposes of this outline, the main difference made between a major sentence and a clause, namely that while both have an S V (C) (A) structure, a clause is itself a component or subcomponent of a larger S V (C) (A) structure. A major sentence on the other hand, however complicated, is not part of a larger S V (C) (A) structure.

In the sentences above, therefore, at various points there are S V (C) (A) structures which are themselves covered by the one description A or S or C as shown. Examples are at A in (v) where 'When the bell rang' can itself be broken down into 'when + S + V', or at C in the same sentence. At C in (v), the structure is, however, even more complicated, since 'books which they had chosen the previous day' is itself a nominal group, structured as h q (h = books, q = which they had chosen the previous day), and it is the q part which is then further broken down into q = which + S + V + A. These subordinate S V (C) (A) structures are clauses operating at different levels in the overall S V (C) (A) structure, which is a major sentence.

Let us set out one of these sentences diagrammatically, and see the various levels at which groups and clauses can occur.

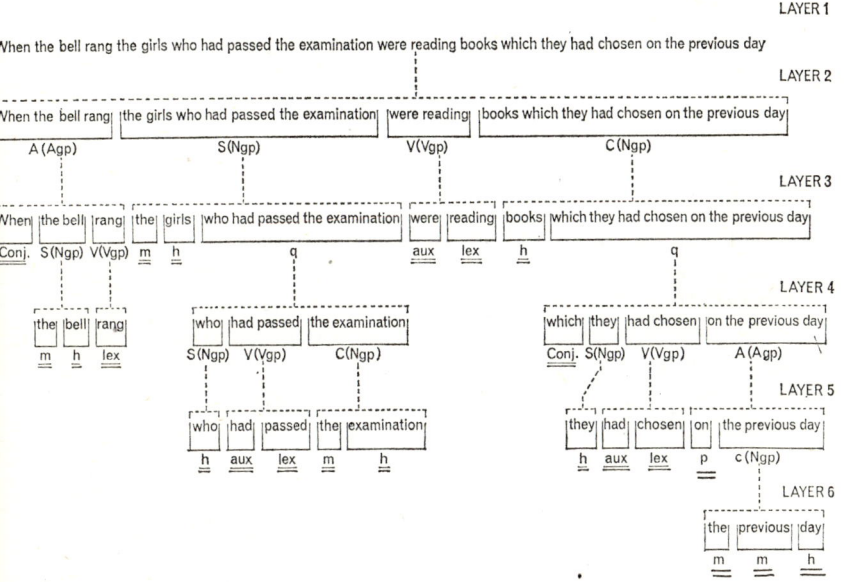

'Cutting' a sentence in this way is often called making an **I.C. (Immediate Constituent) analysis.** The first sentence cut, where the constituents labelled Layer 2 are obtained, results in our seeing that the sentence has four immediate constituents (A S V C). All of these constituents, however, have constituents of their own = Layer 3. Each layer of cutting gives you the immediate constituents of the layer above. When it is no longer possible to make a cut, the **ultimate** constituents are reached indicated in the diagram by double underlining.

In this diagram you will see that I have continued analysing the different structures until only single words are left. It would be quite possible to go on with the analysis down to morphemes. But even restricting the analysis so that the final stage is one of words, you will see that some words (e.g. 'day') are at quite a 'deep' level of patterning. That is, 'day' in this sentence is a part of a nominal group 'the previous day', which is part of an adverbial group, 'on the previous day', which is itself part of a clause 'which they had chosen on the previous day', which again is a constituent in a group 'books which they had chosen on the previous day', which is a constituent of the whole sentence structure. 'Day' is therefore six levels down in the patterning of the sentence.

On page 77 it was said that there is only one S place, one V place and one or two C places in any clause. In sentences (vi), (vii) and (viii), however, there are rather different structures. In (vi) there is at S, in (vii) at C and in (viii) at V structures where the nominal and verbal groups concerned have two or more components at the same level of patterning. In each case here the components are linked by 'and'. 'And', and a limited number of other words (e.g. 'or', 'but', 'sooner than', 'as well as',) always indicate the pattern of **coordination**, i.e. they signify that two or more components are functioning on the same level of structure. There is therefore only one S, V, or C place as the case may be, in sentences (vi)–(viii), but in each, one of the I.C.s (immediate constituents) shows a coordinating pattern within that constituent. In the examples given, the coordination occurs between groups; it can equally well occur between clauses, e.g.:

Lock	the door	when you come in	and	when	you	go out
		conj. S V	+	conj	S	V
V	C		A			

or between words:

Buy	bread and cheese
V	C

SENTENCES—MAJOR AND MINOR

In the paragraphs above, I have been careful to refer to **major sentences**. All the sentences in examples (i)–(viii) were sentences with an S V (C) (A) structure. But look at the following extract from Muriel Spark's *The Bachelors*:

> 'New potatoes in the shops,' Ronald said.
> 'They're always in the shops,' said Martin, 'these days. In season and out of season. It's the same with everything; you can get new potatoes and new carrots all the year round now, and peas and spinach any time, and tomatoes in the spring, even.'
> 'At a price,' said Ronald.
> 'I make do with streaky. I grudge breakfasts,' said Ronald.
> 'Same here.'
> 'Your hand's never out of your pocket,' Ronald said before Martin could say it.

There are various parts of this, such as:
  (i) 'New potatoes in the shops';
  (ii) 'In season and out of season';
  (iii) 'At a price';
  (iv) 'Same here'.

which are perfectly normal parts of a conversation, and which are similar to hundreds of such utterances. Are these utterances sentences? Traditionally, two main criteria for sentences have been set up. The first is that formulated by Otto Jespersen in *The Philosophy of Grammar*:

(*a*) 'A sentence is a (relatively) complete and independent human utterance—the completeness and independence of it being shown by its standing alone or its capability of standing alone, i.e. of being uttered by itself.'

The other is more formally based; and often runs something like this:

(*b*) 'A sentence is a group of words containing a subject and a predicate, which must not be subordinated to a larger construction so as to form a dependent clause.'

This second definition is, of course, the one adopted above to distinguish a clause from a sentence.

The Jespersen definition at (*a*) is difficult to apply to (i)–(iv) above. In what sense are these even relatively complete? 'At a price' could not stand alone in that, if it had not been preceded by another utterance, it would have made no sense at all, any more than say, 'By the cost' would, without a context.

The second definition at (*b*) does not include (i)–(iv) either. These utterances are quite different from the S V (C) (A) structures called either clauses or major sentences above. One common name for the kind of structures we have in (i)–(iv) is **minor sentences.**

A minor sentence is an utterance (which can, of course, be represented in written form), which does not contain a finite verb. A finite verb is one which has to agree in person and number with a subject. Minor sentences (i)–(iv) above do not contain anything recognisable as a verb, either finite or non-finite, but other minor sentences may do so, as for example:

(v) Well done!
(vi) Closed until further notice.
(vii) Damn!

Spoken minor sentences are usually either exclamations, as (v) and (vii), or responses to someone else's utterance, (i)–(iv). Written minor sentences may be representations of either of these, or may be notices, as (vi) above. Sometimes they are used as deliberate descriptive devices, especially where a writer is trying to achieve a special effect as, for example, in this passage:

> Fog everywhere. Fog up the river, where it flows among green aits and meadows; fog down the river, where it rolls defiled among the tiers of shipping and the waterside pollutions of a great (and dirty) city. Fog on the Essex marshes, fog on the Kentish heights.
>
> CHARLES DICKENS, *Bleak House*

In all cases such minor sentences are written between full stops.
To summarise what has so far been discussed:

(*a*) A major sentence has an S V (C) (A) structure which is not itself part of any other S V (C) (A) structure.
(*b*) A clause is an S V (C) (A) structure which is included

within some part of a larger S V (C) (A) structure, i.e. a sentence or another clause.

(*c*) A minor sentence is, in writing, a stretch of language written between full stops, or in speech, is usually either an exclamation or response. Neither in speech nor writing does a minor sentence contain a finite verb.

SENTENCE CLASSIFICATION

Considerable thought has gone into attempted classifications of the different kinds of major sentence, but so far there is little unanimity. Efforts have, in fact, concentrated mainly on the classification of major sentences of a single clause type, and considerable work remains to be done both on these and on the more complicated multi-clausal sentences. One of the more influential classifications has been that of Paul Roberts who in *English Sentences* listed ten patterns (which were not claimed to be exhaustive). It may be of interest to quote these in order to show the lines along which much thought has gone. The clause structure, in our terms, is shown alongside, but this terminology is not used by Roberts.

	Clause structure
1. Subject + intrans. vb. (The ship arrived)	S V
2. Subj. + vb. + adj. (The man seemed young)	S V C
3. Subj. + become / remain } + noun or pronoun (John became a teacher)	S V C
4. Subj. + trans. vb. + noun or pronoun (John ate lunch)	S V C
5. Subj. + vb. of 'give' class + 2 nouns or pronouns (He gave me the book)	S V C C
6. Subj. + vb. of 'consider' class + two nouns or pronouns (We thought him our friend)	S V C C

83

7. Subj. + vb. of 'elect' class + two nouns or pronouns (The class elected John secretary)   S V C C

8. Subj. + 'be' + adverb (John is here)   S V A

9. Subj. + 'be' + adjective (John is angry)   S V C

10. Subj. + 'be' + noun or pronoun (John is a man) S V C

As is apparent, no imperative or interrogative forms are included here, nor does this classification account for sentences such as 'The book cost her five shillings'.

Traditional grammar, such as is still frequently taught, sometimes classified sentences as imperative, interrogative and indicative, and decided where to place any one utterance according to its meaning. This and similar terminology is also used in accounts based on more modern linguistic theory, but no general account of such classifications is available.

Other attempts at classification have included the criterion of pitch movement as part of the information required, and one writer has listed a number of sentence types where classification is based on the order of the elements S and V, the rise or fall of pitch on the last stressed syllable, the presence of 'do', 'does' and/or 'not', and the position of the stress.

The classification of sentence or clause types could, if successful, be very useful for purposes of making comparisons between the ways in which different languages form meaningful patterns, and therefore for devising teaching methods. This forms part of the study of contrastive linguistics. (Chapter 10.)

This chapter has, then, looked in some detail at various units of language patterning; it has been seen that any utterance will consist of morphemes patterned into words, words patterned into groups, groups patterned into clauses, clauses patterned into sentences. The sentences too can be of different kinds, major and minor, and the major and minor themselves comprise many different types. Additional patternings are added by the use of different pitch rises and falls and different intonation contours. Language attains its richness and subtlety by the fusion of these almost infinitely variable patterns with its virtually infinite store of words, infinite because the users of the language will always invent new words when they cannot find old ones to satisfy them. But words without the patterns that display them are poor things, uncut, unpolished gems. The patterning, the grammar, is required to shape, polish and light them. People tend to discuss languages in terms of vocabulary alone, but in English certainly, and in all languages to a greater or lesser extent, the structure or form of the language is the indispensable setting for an effective or aesthetic use of words.

6

Word Meaning

It is only very rarely that it is a simple or easy process to learn, or to teach others, the meaning of a word. With a baby learning to speak one may point to its father and say 'da-da', but for a long time the child will insultingly associate 'da-da' with most adult men. It is only slowly that it realises that 'da-da' refers exclusively to its father, and it is not until this realisation is complete that one can say that the child has 'learnt' the meaning of 'da-da'. A visitor to the Zoo may see a cage with an unfamiliar animal in it, labelled 'lynx', and may thus learn that 'lynx' means a spotted animal with little tufts in its ears. Even this knowledge, however, may be of little use when he reads, a few days later, perhaps in the paperback with which he chooses to pass away his commuting time, 'Lynx-eyed as ever, Steve drew his rifle and cautiously took aim'. The dreary school hours many of us spent learning by rote such things as 'to depreciate' means 'to disparage or belittle, sink or lower in value or price or purchasing power', and 'to deprecate' means 'to advise the avoidance of', or even the hours we spent 'putting these words into sentences', are unlikely to have enabled us to use such words, if we ever do, with any ease or freedom, though a good memory for such exercises and a well-ordered intelligence may have helped us to interpret them when we first met them 'live', as it were.

What, in fact, is the 'meaning' of a word, or words? To answer this with any academic adequacy would require more philosophy and psychology than is here appropriate, but it is at least useful to look at some of the factors which affect, in everyday life and conversation, our understanding of the 'meaning' of words.

Let us first take a particular kind of word whose meaning is apparently simple—a name, defined in *The Pocket Oxford*

Dictionary as 'word by which individual person, animal, place or thing is spoken of or to'. Rationally, most of us are inclined to discount the importance of names ... 'a rose by any other name would smell as sweet' ... but instinctively and emotionally we tend to be more affected than perhaps we care to admit by personal appellations.

Tom, asked if he would like to meet Sophonisba, is likely to be dubious or delighted according to temperament, whereas an invitation to meet Jane or Mary would appear a much more mundane prospect. Most of us can think of names to which we have an automatic revulsion, and many of us have spent many anxious hours selecting names for our offspring. Children themselves have, very early on, decided views about names, as the following quotations show:

> 'My Christian name is Linda. It has no special meaning. I am not named after anyone. I do not like the name because it is common and horrid. Everyone calls me Lynne for short; that isn't bad. If I could choose my name I would choose Samantha because I like it and it is a pretty name as well besides that it is long.'
>
> 'I was christened Stephen Ralph. My second name was named after my great uncle Ralph. I do not like my name because I don't think it's right. I would like to be called Fred because I think it suits me.'
>
> 'My Christian names are Denise Lesley and I think they are horrid. When my father comes home he says where is Fairy-feet. My brothers call me Babs and I asked my mother if she would call me another name like Pat and she said she would not call me anything else. My father said that he likes my name that I have got. My brothers only call me Denise when they want me to go to the shops. When I asked my mother if I could change my name to Pat she said don't be silly and I said I am not silly.'[1]

In some communities considerable religious importance is attached to the use of names; Catholics like to choose appropriate saints' names for their children; some Hindus have a

1. *Where*, No. 33. September 1967.

ritual based on the religious books which will prescribe the initial letter of a child's name. In some Muslim communities it is disrespectful for a woman ever to pronounce aloud her husband's name—an inhibition which, coupled with the absence of surnames, has been known to cause considerable confusion at polling booths, where to my knowledge, several hundred Muslim women all called Shirin, once refused to identify themselves further to the electoral officer by naming their husbands.

ASSOCIATION

So it can perhaps be concluded that logically or not, many people feel that some meaning, some property, other than that of a mere label, attaches to a name. Most of these properties are acquired by **association**; we disliked Aunt Hilda and therefore we came to dislike her label; our first boy-friend was Geoffrey and all Geoffreys tend therefore to enjoy a headstart in our estimation. For most people these associations are purely personal, or at most extend to the immediate family, but some names, of course, because of the fame or notoriety of their holders, have similar associations for great numbers of people. It is a cruel man who would call his child Hitler Smith, and perhaps a slightly old-fashioned one now who fathers Winston Jones.

Many words, other than proper nouns, have commonly recognised associations based on emotional rather than rational attitudes. The dustman, in spite of Eliza Doolittle's father, has had to be renamed a refuse collector in an attempt to enhance his status; a ratcatcher becomes a rodent control officer and the charwoman becomes a lady cleaner, largely because the original names were associated with dirty or menial jobs. Some of us have learnt that a house advertised as 'suitable for a business executive' is likely to cost more than a similar house advertised merely as 'suburban'. Our attitude to racial problems may reasonably be deduced from the choice we make of 'niggers', 'blacks', 'Negroes' or 'Africans' when referring to these people. Whichever of the terms we choose we still refer to the same basic fact, namely a number of human beings with distinctive features and pigmentation, but our choice of words also indicates our own emotional attitude to these human beings. Each of these terms has acquired different associations which for us determine our choice. In the 1950s it was found desirable to amend all the Laws of Kenya by substituting 'African' for 'native' wherever the latter occurred, and even now it is only the sophisticated African who can comfortably use the word 'native' in the factual sense now common in Europe of 'being born in a particular place'. For years it was associated in Africa with the notion of savagery or subservience, as indeed the word has been historically, and was therefore unacceptable to many native Africans.

Words have, in fact, always been recognised as powerful instruments, from the Biblical theme translated (not wholly satisfactorily) as 'In the beginning was the Word, and the Word was with God, and the Word was God' to the modern belief that a man will be more content to do a menial job if only the words which describe it are powerful or impressive enough. In the course of years new words are introduced, old words, along with other aspects of language, change form or meaning, drop out of the language or are revived, but through all the vicissitudes of individual words, one fact remains largely constant; that only in very few cases do two words ever mean exactly the same thing. The search for two words of wholly identical significance is usually vain, the only chance of success being perhaps in cases where words from two separate languages for identical objects exist, at least for a time, alongside each other, as at the time of writing (but possibly for not much longer) do 'gnu' and 'wildebeeste' for the same animal in Kenya, the one a Hottentot, the other an Afrikaans word, but both now assimilated into the form of English used in East Africa.

CONNOTATION

In most other cases the perfect synonym does not exist. An apparent synonym may on examination prove to have a similar or identical **denotation**, but a different **connotation**. That is

D

to say, it may have reference to an identical object or action, but the emotional or other overtones attached to its use may differ. In literature, more than in most uses of language, it is the connotation which is often exploited. Compare for instance the following:

> *Season of mists and mellow fruitfulness!*
> *Close bosom-friend of the maturing sun;*
> *Conspiring with him how to load and bless*
> *With fruit the vines that round the thatch-eaves run.*

> *Season of fog and ripe productivity!*
> *Dear old chum of the developing sun*
> *Plotting with him how to fill and make prosperous*
> *With fruit the vines that under the roof of the thatched house grow.*

Although the rhythm and rhymes are perforce lost in the second version, the structure is for the most part retained, and the ludicrous effect comes largely from the unsuitable connotations of some of the words used.

The connotation a word acquires will depend on a number of factors, most important of which is simply common usage, that is to say the way in which, and the circumstances in which, it is normally used by the majority of native speakers of the language concerned. There is nothing 'wrong' or 'ungrammatical' about the sentence 'His Excellency wishes me to thank you for your great kindness and decency', and the foreigner who wrote it would not seriously be held to be expressing gratitude for the recipient's wearing of an adequate amount of clothing, but the native speaker would not find the colloquial informality he attaches to the use of 'decency' in the sense the writer meant it, as in keeping with the obvious formality of the rest of the sentence. Similarly the schoolboy who writes that 'Macbeth is a smashing great tragedy' is likely to receive instruction in the usage of his own language. The ability to choose words with appropriate connotations is a necessity for anyone who lays claim to any substantial degree of mastery over a language, and it is the more difficult, often neglected stage of learning a foreign language.

To return to literature, it is here that the choice of words with appropriate connotations will often determine the effectiveness of the writing. Consider the following lines, which introduce a description of a picnic on the grass, under some coloured umbrellas:

> The light dripping through these, and cast up again by the rugs and flat stretches of green grass, spattered them with vivid patches of scarlet, purple, blue and sea-green, till they seemed hotly-coloured insects nestling under the shade of a clump of iridescent, rather deleterious toadstools.[1]

The words listed in Roget's *Thesaurus*, as in association with 'spatter' are (amongst others of a similar nature) 'be-smear, begrime, befoul, splash, stain, sully, pollute, smear, etc., etc.'. There is much else to be said about this passage, but 'spatter' already indicates the feelings and attitude towards the characters that the writer wishes to convey. If the first part of the sentence is rewritten substituting only two words for others with similar denotations but different connotations it might run: 'The light falling through these and cast up again by the rugs and flat stretches of green grass, played over them in vivid patches . . .' and the mental, if not physical surroundings become quite different.

One of the difficulties for students studying literature of countries other than their own, is precisely this difficulty of excusable ignorance of word connotation. It can well happen that a connotation is national, based on some social custom or attitude peculiar to one country, so that even where a common language exists, as English between Britain and America, a connotation may not be common. Moreover, a change in social attitudes, or even a variation in attitudes between generations, may make considerable difference in the connotations, for a specific audience, of certain words, and therefore to the significance of the writing as a whole. Take, for instance, the following lines from George Barker's *To My Mother*:

> . . . *Sitting as huge as Asia, seismic with laughter,*
> *Gin and chicken helpless in her Irish hand*

1. Osbert Sitwell, *Triple Fugue.*

'Gin' is a tricky word. It can be used purely factually: 'This factory manufactures gin', but in many circumstances it will also carry overtones. Turning again to Roget (originally compiled we must remember in 1852) we find 'gin' in closest association with 'blue ruin, grog, brandy, port wine' under the heading 'Drunkenness', whereas by contrast, 'whisky' is found under the heading 'Food'. This undoubtedly reflects a social prejudice which has lasted, amongst the older generation in this country at least, almost up to the present day; 'gin' tended to be associated with the lower classes, with debauchery, if only mild. In America, on the other hand, 'gin' (particularly as an ingredient of a Martini) tends to be associated with the wealthier upper classes, while the British connotations of 'gin' tend in some degree to be associated in America with 'bourbon'. Thus even between British and American readers, or between older and younger readers, 'To My Mother' may well convey a different flavour, a different ambience. The British connotation again tends to be strengthened by the collocation (see p. 93) with 'Irish'. This is because to many people—very unjustly no doubt—'Irish' also connotes 'poverty', 'lower classes' and 'fecklessness'. Thus the two words each with similar possible connotations have these connotations strengthened when they are in collocation with each other. The fact that the rest of the poem does much to draw a contrast and to contradict this particular impression, is, for the moment, irrelevant. In the same two lines, however, we have 'seismic', metaphorical, striking and one might think, international. But even here, it is not possible to be sure that 'seismic' does have quite the same connotations in England, where earthquakes are a scientific fact rather than a stark reality, and in, say, Chile, where the connotation must, one would think, be much more violent, and the poem on this account perhaps appears strained and exaggerated.

Sometimes a variation in the final (bound) morpheme will be used to indicate variation in connotation. Thus in English we have the adjectives 'yellowish, yellowing, yellowy'. The morpheme 'yellow' has in itself numbers of possible connotations, depending to some extent on context, but the force of the '-ish', '-y' and '-ing' morphemes are all different. Whereas the pages of an old book might be 'yellowing' or simply 'yellow', they are less likely to be 'yellowish' or 'yellowy'. A sick man's complexion might be 'yellowish' and with both 'yellowish' and 'yellowing' the overtones of the word are likely to be slightly derogatory—to indicate a departure from normal standards. It is probably for this reason that Gerard Manley Hopkins in the following lines chose 'yellowy' which is less common, and lacks the derogatory overtones:

> *Some candle clear burns somewhere I come by*
> *I muse at how its being puts blissful back*
> *With yellowy moisture mild night's blear-all black,*
> *Or to-fro trambeams truckle at the eye.*

It will be realised that connotation is based partly on association with other facts, but also largely on emotion. The emotive use of words is one of the keystones both of poetry and of political propaganda; the use of a word not only to indicate a physical or mental 'fact', but also to suggest the feelings which accompany the fact. That the light 'spatters' instead of 'plays' indicates reactions of heart rather than eyes; a 'nigger' differs from a 'Negro' and a 'German' from a 'Hun' only in the emotional feelings of the speaker. 'A red light' and a 'rosy glow' may in fact be descriptions of the same 'fact' but no one will doubt that the speaker feels, and the hearer is meant to feel, differently towards the 'fact' in each case. Hopkins 'fresh fire-coal chestnut-falls' takes us to another realm of fact. With these examples, however, we are coming on to words, not alone, but in association with other words.

COLLOCATION

A word on its own, a name, a cry is powerful, but words in association with others become infinitely more powerful and subtle and of greater potential depth. The child learns that 'Mummy' is effective, that 'Mummy I want ...' is more so, and that 'Please, darling Mummy, I want ...' is even more productive of results. **Collocation** simply means the 'placing together' of two or more words or phrases. In this sense 'darling Mummy' or 'bad man' are collocations, as is also 'deleterious toadstools'. Whereas some writers prefer to regard collocation as referring to two items which are in actual physical juxtaposition to each other, it is more usual and more profitable for present purposes, to take it as referring to words or phrases which are obviously contextually related, even though not physically juxtaposed. Thus in the example on page 91, 'gin', 'chicken', 'Irish' and 'hand' are all regarded as collocating with each other, and in the sentence 'Colonel Smith, who had endeavoured to listen patiently, now turned purple with rage', 'Colonel Smith' and 'purple' would be regarded as in collocation. A collocation may vary from the wholly expected, e.g. 'burning hot', 'pouring rain' or 'intrinsic value' to the wholly unexpected, e.g. 'vociferous lobster' 'freezing hot' or 'condensed moonlight'. At one extreme the parts of a collocation are wholly predictable (e.g. 'desirable residence' in a house agent's advertisement) and at the other so unpredictable that each part gains new life. The wholly predictable is equivalent to a cliché, the wholly unpredictable may be either a literary inspiration or an advertising gimmick; no merit necessarily attaches to either predictability or unpredictability. To a large extent, the study of 'style' is the study of unpredictability. What is called a 'flat' style[1] is likely to be one where all words and structures are so predictable that they make relatively little impact. On the other hand a 'vivid' style is likely to be one where words or structures are relatively eccentric and therefore arresting. In discussing collocations in literature therefore, what is most usually singled out for comment is the collocation that is unexpected, or which makes some impact, whether by its appropriateness or inappropriateness, its accuracy or inaccuracy. At one extreme there is the simple juxtaposition of adjective and noun, at the other extended metaphor; critical consideration of the 'words' of a piece of literature will include both, and will be given direction by a study of the effect of collocation.

1. For an explanation of the term 'style' as used here, please see Chapter 7, page 109f.

But the study of collocation is of value not only in literature but in many other aspects of language. A study of the development of a child's language will show gradually greater awareness of what normally 'goes with' what, and as a child's vocabulary extends so too must his awareness of what constitutes a 'normal' collocation, i.e. a generally accepted and used one. His unawareness is often what causes an adult to think a child's speech to be refreshing and direct. Words freshly learnt by the child have an innocence and directness normally unavailable to the adult whose use of the same words is enmeshed in the complex associations his longer experience has given him, and it is only when the child collocates such words as if they were wholly untrammelled that they regain for the adult some of their original savour.

In teaching a foreign language a study of collocation will increase the efficiency by which vocabulary can be extended, and may also help to avoid the pitfalls of ridiculous or inappropriate constructions such as 'He resorted to luxury' and 'In democratic countries newspapers are the locomotions and means of freedom of speech'.

Collocation, connotation and association have considerable sociological interest also. Word association tests used by psychologists can reveal much, not only of the individual's own reactions, but also of the nature of the society in which he lives. It does therefore make for considerable difficulty in devising language and intelligence tests across cultures, since words, and situations described in words, have quite different significance in different societies. To take a trivial example, 'breakfast' in England is perhaps most likely to be associated with 'bacon and eggs'. In America perhaps more often with 'coffee and toast' (though it might now be more accurate to say that by his responses to 'breakfast' you could specify with some hope of accuracy what sort of a person the Englishman was!).

A further point to be made about collocation is that words which are collocated often tend to have quite a different meaning from that which they have when not so collocated. They may possibly be called 'idioms' or 'metaphors' but most people use them in their different senses without any awareness

95

of idiomatic or metaphorical use. Adjectives, particularly those of colour, seem most likely to be subject to this multiple use. Consider for example, 'white' and its uses in the following collocations:

White race (usually in fact pinkish-grey); white wine (usually pale yellow or gold); white hot (pinkish-white); white coffee (pale brown); white coal (hydro-electric power); white night (sleepless); white lie (forgivable); white noise (in acoustic engineering) and many others. In each of these cases the experienced speaker has no more difficulty in interpreting the 'white' part of the collocation, in spite of its many and varied possibilities, than the child has in knowing the 'meaning' of 'icecream'. In the case of the child recognition and use of the collocation will almost certainly come before recognition and use of the constituent parts 'ice' and 'cream'. In fact it may be true that for most adults as well as children the constituent parts of 'icecream' have lost their virtue and it now exists as a whole only. Firth suggested that the same might apply to 'ass', so commonly collocated with 'you silly . . .' that it has become almost inseparable. He suggested that even if you said 'An ass has been frightfully mauled at the Zoo' someone is likely to retort 'What on earth was he doing?'[1] The potential associations and collocations of any word are therefore part of its meaning. 'White' does not simply have the denotational meaning in the words of *The Shorter Oxford Dictionary* of 'having that colour produced by reflection, transmission or emission of all kinds of light in the proportion in which they exist in the complete visible spectrum, without sensible absorption, being thus fully luminous and devoid of any distinctive tone'. 'White' also has all the meanings inherent in all its possible collocations.

SEMANTIC FIELD

Words also have another source of meaning; that derived from their **semantic field**. This simply means that any one word derives some part of its meaning from the existence of other words of a similar nature. To be specific, part of the meaning of 'bus' is that it is not a car or a coach; part of the meaning of

1. J. R. Firth, 'Modes of Meaning' in *Papers in Linguistics 1934–51*, O.U.P.

'cottage' is that it is not a mansion, or a mews, or a villa, or any of the other things allied to but not synonymous with it. In a language which has only one word to cover all moving vehicles (e.g. 'gari' in Swahili) that word has a wider range of meaning than one of the words into which it may be translated in, say, English. In describing a woman as 'pretty' we have in mind that she is not beautiful, or handsome, or good looking, and therefore part of the meaning of 'pretty' is that it excludes, at least in some part, these other notions.

In some areas of our society there is a strictly regulated set of terms, use of any one of which quite definitely excludes the others. This is the case, for instance, with words used to designate military ranks; if you are a sergeant, you are, by definition, not a private or a corporal, or a lieutenant or a captain. Part of the meaning of 'sergeant' is that it excludes all other ranks. But sometimes words do not so strictly exclude others, and may indeed overlap, or even have an ambiguous relationship to each other, and it is this potential overlap or ambiguity that is often exploited commercially. A car is the 'Super' model, and therefore one might be tempted to think is 'above', i.e. better than others. Then the wary customer may discover that this manufacturer's range of cars is the 'Super', 'De-luxe' and 'Classic' in ascending order, so that the 'Super' is therefore inferior to the other two models. The manufacturer has chosen his own semantic field, words from which can be interpreted only in the light of knowledge of the whole field. A guidebook listing good restaurants or hotels will probably use a system of classification (e.g. luxury—first class—good) which is useless unless all the terms in the field are known. In this context 'good' has a relative rather than an absolute meaning, and can in fact mean 'rather poor'; its meaning derives wholly from the semantic field in which it operates.

In the last examples it might be argued that the words are being used in a technical sense and that they are, therefore, at least to some extent 'different' words from the apparently identical words used in a 'general' or 'non-technical' sense. This is perfectly true, and is in fact only another way of saying that words may have more than one semantic field. In each case, however, their meaning will derive in part from the existence or non-existence of other words in the particular semantic field which is appropriate.

The range of words in any semantic field will vary according to the culture of the society in which they are used. Thus in English we have a word 'camel' which could be said (at least by a non-zoologist) to have a restricted semantic field in that only 'dromedary', and possibly 'bactrian' are possible alternatives. With 'horse', however, we have a considerable range, e.g. 'nag', 'hack', 'thoroughbred', 'racehorse', 'filly', 'gelding', 'carthorse', etc. In countries where the camel has the economic and social importance that the horse has, or had, here, it should not surprise us to find that many more words exist in the same semantic field as 'camel', each of which derives some part of its meaning from the existence of others. This non-correspondence of semantic fields in different languages does, of course, create many difficulties for the translator. How do you translate 'nag' into a language which has only one word for all kinds of horse? Only, probably, by a qualifying phrase or sentence. As Dr. Johnson said: 'Words change their manners when they change their country.'

The many aspects of word meaning discussed above all themselves overlap. A word operates phonologically and grammatically, as we saw in previous chapters. It also operates by virtue of its denotation, connotations, potential or actual collocations and by virtue of its place in a particular semantic field. All these factors and some others yet to be discussed, operate concurrently so that to 'understand' a word is a complicated process where we are required to synthesise meanings derived simultaneously from many sources. Yet some people still 'teach' meanings from word lists!

7
Varieties of Language

Most of us speak quite differently when we speak to different people; to a child, to a friend, or to a superior at work. With some we are relaxed, with others formal; some are intimates, others are strangers or near-strangers. We even speak differently to the same person when we meet him in different circumstances; at work we use the jargon of the office, on the golf course we switch to the different, more informal jargon of the club-house. And two people addressing a third in similar terms and circumstances will nevertheless each have a quite distinctive way of speaking. Even a 'Hullo' on the telephone is often sufficient to identify the speaker to us. Our speech, and in many ways, our use of speech is as individual to us as our handwriting. Yet even within our own **idiolect**—our own individual speech habits—many of us have mastery of a range of different types of language.

Apart from our appraisal of the factual content of what is said or written, we tend to assess people and situations from the way language is used, and often our subsequent actions and attitudes are determined by such assessments. What is it that causes people to use language in any particular way, and what is it that distinguishes such 'fashions of speaking' one from another? What is it about their use of language that influences us in our assessment of people?

The reasons for such variations, and for our assessment of them, are complex, but it is perhaps possible to isolate some of the more specifically linguistic factors and examine them. Other factors such as gesture, tone of voice, and physical attitude are of importance, but must here be left aside. Matters which we can, and subconsciously do, analyse may include:

(*a*) The **regional** or **social dialect** of the speaker. This tells us where he comes from and what we judge to be his

99

position in the social hierarchy of the community. This dialect may be a question of different words, or uses of words, different grammatical structures, or different pronunciation. Where pronunciation only is concerned, the differences are usually referred to as differences of **accent.**

(*b*) The 'correctness' or otherwise of his vocabulary and grammar.

(*c*) The 'level' of his vocabulary and grammar (i.e. slangy, colloquial, erudite, etc.).

(*d*) The choice he makes of vocabulary and structure in respect of the contents of what he is saying (its appropriateness to the relevant circumstances).

Regional and so-called 'social' dialects play a much more important role in English society than in some others. It was Shaw who said that it was 'impossible for an Englishman to open his mouth without making some other Englishman despise him', and although this is undoubtedly less true than it used to be, there is still much truth in it. Many of the older generation, particularly those who have never moved far from their native areas, tend to be distrustful of, if not to despise, people who 'speak differently'. Suspicion is compounded by lack of intelligibility between speakers of broad and differing dialects. The younger, more mobile generation, brought up to use the local speech, sometimes feel inhibited or ashamed of such local speech habits and tend to try to modify their speech nearer to what they feel is a more acceptable form, though in certain areas of society this situation is now changing radically, as this quotation from *The Sunday Times* of 29th October, 1967, shows:

Some time ago Morely took elocution lessons to try to iron out his Cockney accent. 'It was nothing to do with politics. I did it because I fancied myself on TV. But I didn't have the time, and I realised that—provided I didn't go round dropping aitches—changing my speech would mean losing an asset.'

For many years an Englishman tended to be 'placed' not only regionally, but socially by his accent, though there were quite astonishing inconsistencies in standards of acceptance. On the whole country accents were approved of, even if thought 'quaint'. Those who spoke with, say, a broad Devonshire or

Norfolk accent would tend to be stereotyped by many people as probably 'good', or 'worthy', but also probably semi-educated; dull or amusing according to the particular patronising viewpoint adopted. On the other hand, possessors of town accents— a vigorous Brummagem or Scouse[1] tended to come under suspicion of being limited or ignorant and were probably to be distrusted. These are, of course, extremely sweeping generalisations, but given nothing but an accent to judge by, these seemed to many people to be probable corollaries of the accent. Within the British Isles, it is probably true to say that a Scottish accent was thought superior to an Irish or Welsh one, though the initiated would distinguish even within a 'Scottish' accent and prefer the Edinburgh to the Glasgow variety. (Glasgow is a 'town' in a sense that Edinburgh is not, for the greater industrialisation of Glasgow produces a sociological structure in many ways dissimilar from that of Edinburgh). For no immediately apparent reason Yorkshire enjoyed higher status than Lancashire, though the two are often confused by the Southerner and in general, Northern accents were thought inferior to Southern. Such judgements are usually instinctive and difficult to rationalise; challenged, people usually appeal to some vague aesthetics—'the Birmingham accent is so ugly', or 'the Scottish voices are so soft', but it would be difficult to formulate a rational or even consistent code to account for such tastes.[2] In fact the judgement is not usually based on the attractiveness or otherwise of sounds, but on a much more deep-rooted social prejudice. The sound is merely taken as the outward symbol of some inner reality.

The extent to which stereotyping on such a flimsy basis is sometimes carried can be alarming, and the recent tendency to reject such stereotyping is welcome. A greater readiness at least to postpone judgement on the basis of regional accent is apparent in almost all sections of British society, though this does not extend to all 'foreign' accents, such as Indian English,

1. Birmingham or Liverpool.
2. Gimson, in *Introduction to the Pronunciation of English*, points out: 'This rejection of certain sounds used in speech is not, of course, a matter of the sounds themselves; thus [paint] may be acceptable if it means *pint* but "ugly" if it means *paint*.'

or West Indian English. The B.B.C., where for years any marked regional speech flavour meant almost automatic exclusion from most jobs, now sometimes employs, though not without criticisms from listeners, commentators or news readers with perceptible, if not heavily marked regional accents; university professors, eminent businessmen or other well-known figures now regularly appear, regional accents and all, on the mass media.

It is sometimes thought that it is the entertainment world—particularly that of the pop singers and teenage idols, who have established this trend, but it seems more likely that they have merely followed and perhaps helped to consolidate an existing movement. Music hall artistes for years used regional accents as a source of humour, but such accents remained 'humorous' and not 'acceptable', and in their private lives, many of these artistes would feel constrained to adopt a different way of speaking. It is difficult to say when the change of attitude started; probably a combination of the great movements of population occasioned by the two wars, especially the second, the years in power of Labour governments, some of whose greatest men never modified their regional speech, the greater mobility offered by modern transport systems and greater personal affluence, the influence of radio and television, all these and other factors have tended to break down prejudices in respect of regional speech, though such prejudices are by no means extinct. The reverse is sometimes nowadays true—there is in literature and the arts more especially, something of a cult of the 'working man', and possession of a working class dialect, which is usually a regional-cum-social dialect, can, as the quotation on page 100 shows, sometimes be regarded as an asset. Following the successes of the Beatles Pop group, a 'scouse' accent becomes, at least temporarily, desirable in some quarters of society. The trouble is that this tends to be only the reverse side of the coin of stereotyping. The 'working class man', symbolised by his accent, may now be stereotyped as 'genuine', 'real', in some way 'closer to life' than his non-dialect speaking compatriots.

It is, at this stage, necessary to try to see what in fact constitutes a 'regional dialect', or for that matter, a 'dialect', and to see in what way these forms of speaking diverge from the 'more acceptable' speech referred to above. If language is taken in the terms of some of the earlier chapters, i.e. as composed of sounds, grammatical patterns and words, in what respects do dialects vary? Read this brief dialogue from Scott's *Heart of Midlothian*:

> 'This is a fine scene' [the Duke of Argyle] said to his companion, curious perhaps, to draw out her sentiments, 'we have nothing like it in Scotland'.
>
> 'It's braw rich feeding for the cows, and they have a fine breed o' cattle here,' replied Jeanie, 'but I like just as weel to look at the craigs o' Arthur's Seat, and the sea coming in ayont them, as at a' thae muckle trees.'

Scott has here attempted to represent two different methods of speech—a 'standard' form, and a 'dialect' form. As we saw in Chapter 2, it is difficult to represent sound accurately without phonetic transcription, but certain conventions are available in spelling to represent, if crudely, dialect forms of speech. It is apparent that Jeanie's speech differs from the Duke's in at least two aspects—sounds and words. Consonantal sounds may not be so very different, although Scott's orthography suggests that some are dropped (o' for 'of', a' for 'all') but vowels vary considerably, as is suggested by the spelling of 'weel' and 'craigs'. In fact, of course, dialect vowels are likely to vary considerably more than is indicated in this passage, as listening to any dialect speaker can confirm; dialect pronunciation is more than anything else a question of different vowel sounds. Look again at Hardy's representation of Dorsetshire dialect on page 18 for another example.

Again, Jeanie uses some words that the Duke is unlikely to use—'braw', 'ayont' or 'muckle'. These are recognisable as dialect words, used only in a particular region of the country. 'Feeding', while not necessarily a dialect word, is used here in a way the Duke is not likely to use it, and Jeanie's use may be considered dialectal. Grammatically the two speakers are less divergent, but it is perfectly possible to find examples elsewhere of dialectal grammar. For example, and to keep to the Scottish forms: 'Should auld acquaintance be forgot . . .' where the final morpheme of standard English 'forgotten' is not found, or in Norfolk, 'And this be the head of the mighty Bryant clan', (A. Wesker, *Roots*), where the older English form of the verb is retained. On the whole, however, grammatical variation between dialect and standard is relatively less important.

It is necessary at this stage to specify what is meant by 'standard'. The terms **Standard English** and **Received Pronunciation** are generally used to indicate a way of using English which conforms to the natural or acquired habits of educated people whose speech gives no indication of their regional origins. Neither Standard English nor Received Pronunciation (R.P.) can have any absolute values; since every individual speaker of a language uses that language in a way unique to himself, even within Standard, or R.P., there are enough variations to enable us to identify an individual from his speech, or even his writing. There is, nevertheless, a certain body of relatively homogeneous usage which marks the speech of numbers of educated people as alike, and which is referred to as Received Pronunciation (in reference to speech sounds) and Standard English (in reference to word usage and grammatical forms.)

However, it must be realised that this kind of English is itself a dialect; in origin it is the dialect of the upper classes of south-east England; or more specifically of the London area. Over the last few hundred years it has gradually spread outwards from this region, and downwards in the social scale, so that it no longer has a recognisable regional or social provenance, but it is nevertheless still only a dialect which has been to some extent artificially fostered and encouraged. A fact not always realised, moreover, is that this Standard English is spoken today only by a very small minority of the world's English speakers, and that in addition to what we might call Standard British English, there are also dialects which can be, and sometimes are, given such names as Standard Jamaican English, Standard South African English, and so on. Such other 'Englishes' diverge to a greater or lesser extent from Standard British English; at the extremes there may be problems of mutual intelligibility between, say, a Nigerian English speaker and an Indian English speaker, especially if such speakers have any markedly idiosyncratic forms of speech over and above national variations.

A linguist will not regard R.P. or Standard British English as 'better' in any respect than any other regional or national dialect; it is simply another dialect requiring description and analysis in the same way as any other, though its peculiar social and educational status may cause it to be studied more often and in greater depth than other English dialects. The question of 'better' or 'good' speech generally, is a social, and not a linguistic question. Most people in Great Britain do, however, recognise Standard English and to a lesser extent, Received Pronunciation, as linguistic models on which to base the teaching of English, and these models are also commonly used in the teaching of English overseas, at least in those countries which have had close connections with Great Britain.

Social judgements do of course, as we have seen before, impinge on language use, and it is social judgements that cause us to have to distinguish, as linguists, 'social' dialects as well as 'regional' dialects. The two, however, are at most levels closely interconnected, so that to some extent it is misleading to distinguish two different types, 'regional' and 'social', rather than talking of 'socio-regional' dialects. But in so far as they can be distinguished, we might say that whereas regional dialects usually involve kinds of pronunciation, vocabulary and grammar which are distinct from R.P. and Standard English, social dialects to a greater extent constitute varieties of language within either R.P. or regional speech. Certain forms of speech may be thought of as 'upper class' or 'lower class', but it is as well not to be too insistent on the notion of social dialect; what is in this context labelled 'lower class' is likely to be based on regional characteristics, whereas 'upper class' is probably a variant of Standard, or R.P. Anyone who does not speak a regional dialect speaks Standard English; he may, of course, speak Standard English with a regional accent—meaning that his grammar and vocabulary are Standard, but his pronunciation bears some marks of dialect speech. Variations within Standard are as often a question of register and style (see below) as of a specific dialectal variation. It is true that there are certain vowels and certain intonations which are commonly thought of as 'upper class', but again, nowadays, this is often a question of age group rather than of class. The notion of social dialect is still marginally valid, but is of decreasing value in a country probably becoming more class-levelled, or rather perhaps, where class is changing its criteria.

Social judgements of 'good' or 'better' speech usually hinge on what is thought to be the linguistic idea of 'correctness'. You will often be told that such-and-such a form is 'correct'. If asked to state on what authority it is 'correct', people tend to be irritated—it *is* correct—that's what English is like. If pressed, they may refer to some reference book such as the Dictionary, or Fowler. The Dictionary will, in fact (if it is a good one) often refute their claims, though Fowler may be more accommodating. There is a general feeling that somewhere, somehow, there is a body of knowledge which lays down immutable rules for 'correct' English. In fact, of course, no such body exists, and attempts to set one up would be doomed, in the face of the inexorable changes which constantly take place in any language. For example, to insist on the 'correct' use of 'whom' in the spoken language is now anachronistic, for even the most educated speakers rarely use it; to teach that 'aggravate' must be used only in the sense of 'to make worse' is to fly in the face of the commonly accepted practice of the majority of educated speakers of English. In spite of this, certain forms of language are, as we saw on the previous page, recognised by common consent as linguistic models for English, and grammar books are constantly produced which claim to incorporate these models. Such 'grammars' will be dealt with more fully in the next chapter.

But if linguists reject the idea of absolute standards of 'correctness', it nevertheless remains true that certain forms are considered more appropriate than others for particular circumstances. As with dialects, the linguist observes and takes note of the social judgements involved but does not himself pass such judgements. He observes and records that in certain situations this or that form of speech will be used, and not some other; he will note that the forms of speech will vary according to the speaker, the hearer and the circumstances in which both find themselves. Let us go back to Mr. Smith and listen to him speaking first to his wife, then to a colleague, and then to the boss:

(*a*) 'Met that fool John today. Wants his job back—can you imagine?'

(*b*) 'Do you remember John Jones? I met him today and he said he'd like his job back. I think he's optimistic, don't you?'

(*c*) 'I met Mr. Jones yesterday, sir, who used to work here, if you remember? He asked me to inquire whether his post was still open and whether there was any chance of his taking it up again. I said I would pass the message on, sir.'

Each of these three utterances conveys fundamentally the same factual information, but the differing relations of Smith with his wife, colleague and boss cause him to express the information in rather different language forms. The decreasing degree of intimacy in the three sets of circumstances causes him to become increasingly formal and to use markedly different vocabulary and structure. When language is varied in this way, we say that the speaker has moved from one **register** to another. A register is defined as 'a variety of language distinguished according to use', whereas a dialect is a 'variety of language distinguished according to user.'[1]

Apart from the registers illustrated above, Mr. Smith will master many others. He may, for instance, in his office also say to the boss:

(*d*) 'The net result is a deterioration in margins, from 10·9 per cent to 10·3 per cent. If we break down the third quarter figures we can pinpoint the trouble. Profits fell in the third quarter in several sectors . . .'

Or to his colleague he may say over coffee:

(*e*) 'I used a wide-angle lens at 1/100th with aperture at

1. Halliday, McIntosh and Strevens, *The Linguistic Sciences and Language Teaching* Longmans.

ƒ8. I think the graininess must be due to the film not the exposure or the processing . . .'

And to his wife, when in less genial mood he may say:

(ƒ) 'I think it's about time the children learned that I expect them to make less noise when I'm trying to read the newspapers . . .'

All such samples could properly be described as belonging to yet different registers.

There are cases in which a person using different varieties of language for different uses will in fact use different languages. In Kenya, it is not uncommon to hear a student speak to a lecturer in English, to a friend in Kikuyu and to the hall-porter in Swahili all within the space of five or ten minutes. Even those of us, however, who master fluently only one language, have varieties of language for different purposes, some of which were illustrated above. These were different varieties of one person's speech. The notion of register can, however, be extended over many more varieties of language, and these varieties can be classified in a number of different ways. One may, for instance, distinguish registers according to the medium employed—technically, the **mode** of discourse. The main division to be recognised here is that between speaking and writing. The spoken mode has of course many subdivisions, such as conversation, lecturing, commanding, 'phatic' communion, and so on. The written mode has many more; journalism, scientific writing, legal language, and so on. One might wish to add the classifications of reading and reciting as main headings, or they could be regarded as sub-categories of either writing or speaking.

Cutting across such a classification is another which distinguishes the nature of the topic around which the language activity is centred, technically, the **field** of discourse. Here one might make categories such as Technical, Domestic or Social, and might subdivide into such things as biology, chemistry, linguistics, economics under 'Technical'; or parent–child, housekeeper–tradesman under 'Domestic'; or 'phatic', friendly, business–social under 'Social'; and so on according to the particular field. Such categories will inevitably overlap with another classification which can be drawn according to the relations between the people talking or writing to each other, where one's main categories might be Formal and Informal, with the subsequent sub-categories of superior–inferior, social equal, man–woman, and so on. Such a classification would be said to be according to the **tenor** of the discourse.

It is obvious that there is considerable overlap in all these classifications and across them. But it is quite possible for an individual to switch, even mid-sentence, from one register to another. Such switches are apparent—and they are apparent because of changes, however slight, in vocabulary, structure and intonation. It is not possible here to discuss the characteristics of different registers in any depth; but most of us recognise without difficulty some of the more hackneyed examples. The Written mode, Scientific field, Formal tenor, for instance, is normally associated with a high percentage of passive voice constructions, as well as with scientific vocabulary:

'It will be readily understood from the foregoing that the yield point and ductility, particularly of ferrous metals, may be greatly modified by the treatment, often involving great strains, which metals undergo during manufacture, such, for example, as rolling or drawing while cold.'

On the other hand, the Spoken mode, Shopping field, Formal tenor, is commonly associated with a high proportion of interrogative forms, and with certain forms of address not commonly found elsewhere:

'Would Madam like to try the blue one on?'

Much of what has been said here about registers will of course strike familiar notes with anyone who has ever discussed 'style', and it may be wondered what the value is of apparently coining a new name for an old dog. 'Style' is, however, a protean word, which is used in so many different ways by so many different writers that it is now difficult to use it with any technical sharpness. As usual, there is no unanimity among linguists about terminology, or even about the concepts behind the terminology, but it is convenient here to use 'register' in the way indicated above. What has been called 'tenor' of discourse above is called 'style' of discourse by some linguists. In general it seems more useful to keep to 'register' and 'tenor' and to reserve 'style' for that personal element of language which marks out one writer or speaker from another. It is apparent that any two writers using, say, the Written mode, sub-category Journalism, similar fields (e.g. both describing the same train crash), and the Formal tenor of discourse will yet both produce quite different stretches of language. In so far as the differences do not relate to different objective facts, or to the differences demanded by the particular requirements of the intended readers, they are likely to be differences of personal style.

No comprehensive categorisation of registers is yet available, though most people frequently use the ideas behind any such potential categorisation, even if in crude form. Every time we insist on a letter which starts 'Dear Sir' ending with 'Yours faithfully', rather than 'Yours affectionately', every time we tell a child not to use slang in an essay; every time we hesitate as to 'how best to put it' to the boss; every time we decide to telephone rather than to write, we are making decisions on the basis of the selection of the appropriate register for our purpose. There are signs that work may be forthcoming from linguists on this topic; a recent article, 'Aspects of Varieties Differentiation' by Gregory in the *Journal of Linguistics*[1] points out that the fears concerning the difficulties may be unfounded, and goes on to suggest methods of approach. But a rigorous categorisation of varieties of language is a highly technical process which will have to take its place in the queue along with the mass of other research waiting to be done on language problems. Useful preliminary material is likely to be afforded by work on some of the Nuffield projects such as the Child Language Survey, the Foreign Language Teaching Materials project and the Linguistics and English Teaching programmes. Also, of course, the massive research project under Professor Quirk at University College, London, on the Survey of Educated English Usage will afford invaluable material.

1. Volume 3, No. 2, October 1967.

Meanwhile, are there any practical implications in considering, from the layman's angle, the question of varieties of language within any one language? We have seen already that the regional or social variety of language used by a speaker may affect the social judgements passed upon him, and it is equally true that the choice he makes of varieties within his dialect will also have personal and sociological results. Even if to the linguist there is no 'correct' grammar, society decides upon 'appropriate' grammar and penalises the person who chooses 'I were that tired . . .' rather than 'I was so tired . . .', just as it penalises the child who writes for the teacher in a way the teacher considers inappropriate to the circumstances. The choice of 'appropriate' register may seem, with most educated people, almost instinctive, but it has in fact been learned, one way or another, since birth.

Some of us, however, have less explicit and less adequate chances than others of learning in this field. While this is obvious in the more superficial reaches—such as those exemplified above, it now seems likely that there are much deeper implications for the individual in his access to different linguistic forms. Perhaps one can drill the ambitious man not to drop his aitches (or more likely he drills himself), or the child with an examination to pass can be drilled into certain more acceptable forms of language over a restricted examination-orientated range, but the real problems lie much deeper. They have been explored in some depth by psychologists such as Piaget, Vyogtsky and Luria and by sociologists such as Bernstein.

Bernstein's work is of considerable interest in terms of varieties of language. His best-known ideas have revolved around the notions of the use of **restricted** or **elaborated codes** of language used. To quote his own summary:

> . . . it will be argued that a number of fashions of speaking, frames of consistency, are possible in any given language and that these fashions of speaking, linguistic forms, or codes, are themselves a function of the form social relations take. According to this view, the form of the social relation or—more generally—the social structure generates distinct linguistic

III

forms or codes and *these codes essentially transmit the culture and so constrain behaviour.*[1]

The thesis is that any one language can afford a speaker a number of different ways of using the language—there are a number of 'fashions of speaking'. Which 'fashion' a speaker adopts is likely to be decided mainly by his social experiences, but in turn his 'fashion of speaking' determines his social relationship to other speakers and to objects. His social behaviour is constrained within the limits set by his linguistic behaviour, which is in its turn constrained by his social experience. A child who has access, probably because of a favourable home environment, to many different 'fashions of speaking' will therefore be able to operate in many more contexts and with greater freedom and success than the child who has access to only a limited number of such speech systems. Of such different speech systems, or linguistic codes, Bernstein distinguishes two general types—restricted, and elaborated.

The essence of the difference between a restricted and an elaborated code is the predictability (by a linguist or other trained observer) of the language elements likely to be selected by the speaker. In the case of a restricted code, the speaker will choose from a limited set of alternative ways of organising his language to convey meaning; in the case of an elaborated code, the speaker will have a much larger range of alternative language elements from which to choose in order to convey meaning. With a restricted code, therefore, it is obvious that the chances of predicting which language elements are used will be much greater. A restricted code is not necessarily simple, and a speaker using a restricted code may speak at great length, but the forms of language used will be restricted in kind. A church service, for instance, may be almost wholly predictable both as regards vocabulary and structure, but the language, although predictable, is not simple. Equally a set of regulations concerning say, safety in mines, may be complex, but based on a restricted code. On the other hand, a short poem may use an

1. 'A Socio-linguistic Approach to Social Learning' in *Penguin Survey of the Social Sciences* 1965.

elaborated code where both vocabulary and structure are very largely unpredictable. It is probably true to say that anyone who uses elaborated codes of language can, and does, use restricted codes frequently, and for well-defined purposes. On the other hand, the person who because of social experience (or lack of it) rarely hears, or is encouraged to use, elaborated codes, will have difficulty in conveying meaning in any other than restricted and conventional codes. If it is true, as Bernstein holds, that '. . . distinct linguistic forms—fashions of speaking—induce in the speakers *different* ways of relating to objects and persons', it becomes obvious that speakers of differing codes will, within the same general culture, become separated and divided by their differing outlooks. Possession of a common 'language'—e.g. 'English'—is often thought to be a unifying factor between peoples. And in a broad sense this is undoubtedly true—the fact that in England, North America and Australia, as well as many other countries, the people for the most part speak English as the mother-tongue, undoubtedly gives them a strong bond in common; nevertheless, within the bonds of 'English' the variety of ways of using this English is a divisive factor. As a child masters language, he masters his social environment and its requirements; when his language affords him only limited ways of orientating towards this environment his reaction with that environment is likely also to be limited. A person with a larger number of linguistic codes at his disposal can switch from one social role to another with greater ease, and can adapt with greater flexibility to the varying demands of different situations.

The interest of Bernstein's theories is primarily sociological, and this necessarily superficial account cannot do more than refer to some of the theories which can undoubtedly be of great interest to linguists; as with so many other aspects of this type of research, however, full confirmation of the theories is likely to have to await the collection and analysis of much larger samples of data—of actual language in use. But the main theory is attractive if only because it seems to offer some answer to the sort of problems recognised when people say things like: 'So-and-so doesn't get any further because he is so inarticulate . . .'

or 'Johnny is basically intelligent but he just can't communicate adequately ...' It would seem that Bernstein is seeking to systematise and formalise such judgements and to seek reasons in society for their existence.

We can perhaps see, then, that to say that a person 'speaks English' (or French, or Japanese) is to use a blanket term, useful but deceptive. Put another way, some of us speak more English than others. We have an implicit recognition of this situation when we talk about a new colleague: 'You'll like him, he speaks the same language as us.' We mean that his cast of mind, his approach to life, is like ours. As so often, common, intuitive recognition has preceded, in this saying, the sometimes convoluted arguments of social scientists and psychologists.

8

Language, Grammars and People

A parlour game has recently been played on television where three or four people interested in literature listen to the reading of a short extract from some book, and then try to say who wrote the passage and in what book. This is of course a variant of the 'context' questions many of us were, or are familiar with in literature examinations in school. Sometimes the participants in this programme think aloud, allowing us to see how they reach their conclusions. Typical comments have been something like this:

'The key word is "communists"—must be this century'
'The innumerable qualifications in that first sentence—must be Henry James—or a parody of James?'
'A list—Belloc liked lists . . .'
'Not a modern writer—the style is nineteenth century.'

A difficult exercise we may think, and are perhaps astonished at how often the answers are right.

But most of us perform similar exercises fairly frequently. You hear a woman sitting behind you in the underground asking someone whether the train goes to Charing Cross, and without turning round you could probably deduce whether she is a native of northern or southern England, or elsewhere, roughly how old she is, and possibly how well educated; you might be able to tell whether she is a stranger to London or whether she just didn't see the train indicator before she got on and the doors shut, and very likely you could say something about her temperament too—worried, placid, anxious, carefree? Or a schoolboy turns on the radio and hears a snatch of dialogue, perhaps something like this:

'For ever and ever, my sweet, I promise you'
'I can't believe anyone has ever been so happy before'

and he snaps it off with some comment such as 'Another soppy love story!'

Disembodied, brief snatches of language yet have much to tell us about those who use them. They have this power because we already have an extensive knowledge of society and language is essentially social. A knowledge of our society will enable us to predict with some degree of accuracy the probability of certain kinds of language being used in any particular situation, and conversely given a stretch of language, we can predict with some reliability the social situation out of which it arose. No language exists independently of people; it is doubtful if an isolated individual human, however innately intelligent, would ever speak unless in the environment of other speakers. Accounts of circumstances where children have survived without other humans appear to confirm this supposition. Language is necessary to society for many reasons, some of which were discussed in Chapter 1; equally society is necessary to language and to attempt to study language without society is like studying anatomy without a body.

Much study of language, especially in Europe in the nineteenth century, was devoted to working out how particular languages had changed and developed, and how different languages were related to each other. In other words, linguistic study was mainly historically orientated. It is really only in this century that any great effort has gone into studying language as it exists at any one point in time, usually the present. Partly this was because of the difficulty, which soon became apparent, of selecting the material for such a study. To study, say, English as it exists in April 1968, it is not wholly satisfactory to take that English spoken by Mr. A., aged 45 years, living in Wolverhampton, or London, or wherever it happens to be. But if not this English, then how can one ascertain what does constitute English in April 1968? And even assuming that some satisfactory method of doing this was achieved, it would be necessary to work out the relationship between Mr. A.'s English and English in general. An early theoretical approach to these problems was made by the linguist de Saussure, who postulated three kinds of 'language'. French fortunately afforded terms not so readily available in English, and the French words are still usually used in discussing his ideas. De Saussure recognised 'la parole', that is, roughly, the use to which any one speaker puts 'la langue', which is the corporate behaviour, linguistically speaking of all speakers who are mutually comprehensible. Then there was 'le langage', which is language in general, all language found everywhere in every written or spoken form, past or present. De Saussure, in discussing these ideas, suggested that it would be impossible to study 'le langage', which he said, would be 'inconnaissable'. But 'la langue' can only exist through the existence of numbers of people, and in studying 'la langue' one perforce studies at least some aspects of these people. Moreover, we cannot meaningfully study Mr. A.'s English (la parole), without studying its relationship to English (la langue), and therefore to other people. Mr. A.'s English is meaningless except in the context of all English. To study 'la parole' without 'la langue' may be as rewarding as studying the gestures of a single ape in a cage at the Zoo. Not all linguists however, agree with de Saussure's ideas, as will be seen, for example, in a later discussion of the basis of transformational grammar.

Go to a foreign country where you understand not a word of the language spoken around you. If you gradually succeed in 'picking up' the language, it is because you hear on a number of different occasions, from different speakers, certain sounds in particular circumstances which allow you, eventually, to deduce their meaning. Such sounds are used by people who obtain certain effects by using them to other people at certain times and places. By observing the social context and listening to the noises, you learn the meaning. In complementary fashion, one cannot be said to know fully the meaning of any part of language without knowing the social context in which it may, or does occur. To look up a French word list and find that 'fille' = 'girl or maid' is to have only a very partial knowledge of the meaning of the word.

The theoretical nature of the link between language and society is increasingly being studied by psychologists, sociologists and linguists. Stimulus to such research has come from a

117

number of sources, but one of the most influential, at least in this country, was the work of Malinowski, an anthropologist, and J. R. Firth, a linguist who is now thought of as the founder of what has been termed the 'British school' of linguistics. Firth, in an article in *The Sociological Review* of 1950[1], said that he and his group '[studied] language as part of the social process' and that a 'key concept' to their technique was the concept of the **context of situation,** deriving from Malinowski's use of the term as being 'a bit of the social process which can be studied apart'. Firth believed that this context of situation could be studied not as a vague, shifting background to a language event, but more rigorously in terms of a group of 'related categories at a different level from grammatical categories but rather of the same abstract nature'. He did not elaborate, but did suggest that such categories could be:

(*a*) the relevant features of participants; persons, personalities.
    (i) the verbal action of the participants.
    (ii) the non-verbal action of the participants.
(*b*) the relevant objects.
(*c*) the effect of the verbal action.

Even those linguists who have accepted the general thesis, have done little to follow up this line of approach, daunted no doubt by the immense difficulties of any such categorisation. Tentative attempts have been made but on the whole it has been felt more important to work first at the perhaps rather more accessible grammatical and lexical categories necessary to an adequate description of the language. Nevertheless, thinking about language has been greatly influenced by the context of situation theory.

If thinking about language has been influenced by this theory, so also has thinking about psychology and sociology been influenced by the study of language. Sociologists such as Bernstein have studied language in a way which allows it a highly important part in social analysis, and more particularly in the

1. 'Personality and Language in Society', *The Sociological Review*, xlii 2, reprinted in J. R. Firth, *Papers in Linguistics 1934–51*. O.U.P.

consideration of problems of educatability. Psychologists such as Piaget and Vygotsky, in studying the development of the child, have been very concerned with the development of its language. Linguistic study can contribute very materially to psychological and sociological work, but the studies of **psycholinguistics** and **sociolinguistics** are still, for the most part, studies of psychology or sociology. Advances in linguistics will, however have considerable relevance to the way in which these other associated fields are studied. For example, if it is accepted that it is the linguist's job to determine what is learned, and the psychologist's job to determine how it is learned, it is likely that the linguistic formulation will have considerable influence on the formulation of a description of the learning process. This influence can perhaps be seen when the distinctions between two currently popular ways of looking at language are considered.

In America in recent years, the greatest interest and effort has gone into the formulation and refining of **generative** grammars, while elsewhere the emphasis has been on **descriptive** grammars. A descriptive grammar, basically, sets out to analyse and classify existing language, and to set up criteria for determining such classification. In order to analyse and classify, it takes its material from some **corpus**, i.e. it collects samples of language (spoken or written) which have been produced by speakers or writers in the (usually immediate) past. Its description is therefore based on actual, existing language. A generative grammar however, seeks to develop a set of rules which will, by their operation, explain how grammatically acceptable stretches of language are produced, or can in future be produced, and which will enable an evaluation to be made to determine whether a stretch of language which has been produced does fit into the grammar of that language. The two types of grammar are obviously not mutually exclusive, and can, at least in theory, be translated into one another. In so far as a psychologist makes use of a generative or descriptive grammatical model however, his techniques and assumptions must necessarily be modified.

The term 'grammar' has been rather freely used above,

without specifying what in fact is meant by it. The term may easily be misleading and it might be helpful to set out more specifically what is meant by 'grammar'. A common everyday use of the word is in collocation with 'bad': 'You can't say that, it's bad grammar'. Again, school timetables sometimes have periods labelled 'English Grammar' or simply 'Grammar'. The sort of grammar implied here is likely to be primarily **prescriptive** grammar, i.e. something which will lay down rules determining whether or not a particular arrangement or use of language is 'correct', according to some, usually undefined, standard. In the same category come texts which are designed to help the student to learn a language other than his own native tongue. 'English grammar for foreign students' will probably (or certainly should) be rather differently designed from 'English Grammar' designed for native speakers, but both, either implicitly or explicitly, set up certain 'norms' or standards to which 'good' speech or writing is expected to conform.

Modern grammars attempt to be **scientific.** A scientific grammar will attempt to provide a logical and self-consistent account of how language works; it attempts for instance, to answer the problem set out on p. 75, i.e. to explain how the constructions: 'He started to read' and 'He started reading' are related, and how their relationship is so different from the superficially similar constructions: 'He wanted to wash' and 'He wanted washing' where the underlying relationship is obviously very different. A scientific grammar makes no pronouncements of whether any piece of language is 'correct' or not. It is however, apparent that for a grammar of type (*a*)— a prescriptive grammar—to be of any use, it must be founded on a satisfactory grammar of type (*b*).

Within the category of scientific grammars however, there are a number of possibilities. The one on which most of us were brought up was what is now called **traditional grammar.** Traditional grammar has a solid theoretical basis. Those who formulated it sought to discover logical rules of syntax and usage, relying heavily on their own intuition for understanding the rules. Unfortunately their attempts at discovering these rules were, or became, vitiated by some of their assumptions. One assumption they made, for instance, was that language didn't, or shouldn't change. Where change occurred, it was 'corruption'. From this attitude arose the straitjacket of prescriptive grammars which attempted to keep the language in its pure and 'incorrupt' form. Another assumption they made was that Latin was the 'most logical' of languages, and should therefore serve as a model for all descriptions of language. Thus English was described in terms of Latin grammar. It may perhaps be surprising that this should be possible at all, since the origins of English, as we shall see in Chapter 11, have only an indirect relationship with Latin, and one might expect the two grammars to have little in common. In fact much English grammar could (and can) be described in terms of a relationship of grammatical categories which is not dissimilar from the relationships within Latin grammar, and there has recently been considerable discussion about whether there is in all languages, not just Latin and English, a common underlying system of relationships which can be described in similar grammatical terms. However that may be, the efforts of the traditional grammarians to make English fit into the now petrified systems of Latin grammar were bound to result in distortion at least on the superficial layers of description.

It became apparent that a new theory of grammar was required, as distinct from a new grammar, and linguistics in its modern sense has been largely concerned with the search for a new theory, and with attempts to construct a grammar on a theoretical basis which would be sounder than the 'Latin logic' of the traditionalists. In searching for such a theory, it was natural in this century to look at the sciences, and see if help was forthcoming there. Those sciences which are based on observation of existing material usually analyse this material by making abstractions. Those parts of the material which appear similar will be considered together and typified. When the material is thus sorted, then relationship between the various 'types' will be considered, and each 'type' further studied to achieve further abstractions. To give a crude example: in studying animals one might isolate as a 'type' the 'feline' animals, as opposed to the 'canine', etc. The relationship, if any, between felines, canines and others will be considered, as will also the further grouping of felines into lions, tigers, wild cats, domestic cats and so on, and further classifications are made until one eventually reaches the individual cat. Linguistic analysis came to be thought of as a similar kind of empirical science, in which one could make abstractions of constant elements, and could show the relationships between all the members which composed a particular 'type' and between the different 'types'.

There has been much argument over whether the linguists' abstractions are a reflection of something inherent in the actual material of the language, or inherent in the speaker's mind (popularly known as the 'God's truth' theory) or whether the abstractions are wholly fictitious, existing only as part of the linguists' necessary tools for coping with the task of linguistic analysis (popularly known as the 'hocus-pocus' theory). From a linguist's point of view the latter is the easier theory to work with, since the other view might imply an approach through such disciplines as physiology, neurology or psychology, which are not yet equipped to give us any real guidance on linguistic analysis. Moreover, a linguistic analysis which, starting from language, is capable of fulfilling the scientific criteria of being consistent, exhaustive and economical would seem to be satisfactory in itself.

A 'structural' view of linguistics thus took shape, analogous to other sciences where abstractions were made of constant elements, and relationships between them stated. **Structural linguistics** relied on formal criteria for these abstractions. In its more excessive manifestations it tried to exclude the study of meaning; it preferred to look at form and substance and ignore meaning because it was thought to be impossible to describe it. Structuralism might be summarised as saying that it sought to explain the working of language in terms of the functions of its components and their relationship to each other. First it was necessary to isolate the various kinds of components, then to analyse their composition in such a way as to enable a generalisation to be made concerning their internal structure, and then to relate these components and subcomponents in terms of their function in the total structure of which they formed part. The immediate constituent analysis described on pp. 79–80 is based on this sort of grammar.

As has been mentioned, a rather different kind of scientific grammar has more recently been developed in America. This is a generative grammar of the kind described on p. 119 and based on **transformation** theory. The theory is primarily associated with the work of Noam Chomsky at the Massachussetts Institute of Technology. Underlying this theory is the concept developed by the transformationalists of the notions of **competence** and **performance.** These are allied to de Saussure's ideas of 'la langue' and 'la parole', but Chomsky rejects de Saussure's ideas of 'la langue' as a body of material, or an inventory of items from which the individual speakers selects 'la parole'. Instead, Chomsky sees language as consisting of the speaker, or hearer's inner knowledge of his language (competence) and his actual use of language in concrete situations (performance). Competence is an underlying generative process which will find ever more possible acts of performance. Although very little is really known of the process and how it is achieved, we can see from common observation that a child at quite an early age, say five or six, uses language in a way which shows a high degree of powers of generalisation. He can produce thousands of sentences he has never before heard. He has, in other words, produced for himself, an internal 'grammar' which permits the formation of new material. This is his linguistic competence. What in fact he actually says, will depend not only on this competence, or internal grammar, but also on other factors such as his physical or mental state of health, his emotions, the pressure under which he is speaking and many other linguistic and non-linguistic factors. Performance is fundamentally derived from, and influenced by, competence, but the two are different in kind and in function. If this is correct, it implies of course, a study of language at different stages; the stage of competence, which lies deeper and must be explained as the probably innate, generative knowledge which enables speakers to manipulate or to produce 'new' language, and the stage of performance which lies nearer the surface, and is the external manifestation by one, or many speakers and hearers, of the operation of the rules of the grammar of competence.

It can be seen then, that the crucial difference between the structuralist and the transformationalist approach to grammar is that while the former is trying to describe something which is at least theoretically (and temporarily) fixed or static, the latter attempts to illuminate the way in which any particular piece of language is created, by '[characterising] the intrinsic tacit knowledge or competence that underlies actual performance'[1]

Thus a structuralist grammar may describe two different states of the language, e.g. may describe (*a*) 'the man bought a dog', and (*b*) 'the dog was bought by a man', while transformational grammar will be concerned with a set of rules which can produce (*b*) from (*a*). This aim is often achieved in linguistic descriptions based on transformational grammar with great precision and clarity. Even complex operations can be described with great explicitness and it is indeed this explicitness which is one of the attractions of transformational grammar. But it has considerable limitations for other linguistic uses, such as the describing of a text, or a literary comparison of style. Once too, the early 'rules' are absorbed, one soon becomes swamped in complexities which arise from its claim to be 'fully explicit', a claim which sometimes, perhaps unfairly, seems to result in large sledge hammers being used to crack very small nuts. As Gleason commented 'The transformational-generative model is not efficient on a restricted scale. It is like a diesel engine—fine for heavy duty, but hopeless to run a motor scooter'.[2] We have no space to deal with the complexities of this particular diesel engine and its duties, but a list of books dealing with these theories, and with structural theories, will be found at the end of the book. It is interesting to see that in many ways, modern transformational thinking has greater affinity with the ideas of philosophers such as Descartes, A. W.

1. N. Chomsky *Aspects of the Theory of Syntax*. M.I.T.
2. H. A. Gleason *Linguistics and English Grammar*. Holt, Rinehart Winston.

Schlegel and especially Wilhelm von Humboldt, than with the linguistic thinking of the later nineteenth and early twentieth centuries.

A further, British, theory of how language works, is often referred to as the **scale and category** theory. This is primarily associated with the work of Professor M. Halliday and other people who studied under, or were influenced by the work of J. R. Firth. This theory recognises four basic, interrelated **categories** which between them will account fully for all linguistic material (i.e. all observed speech or writing), and a set of **scales** of abstraction which relate these fundamental categories to the linguistic material and to each other. The four fundamental categories are labelled **Class, System, Unit** and **Structure**, and the scales are those of **Rank, Exponence** and **Delicacy**. A description of any one language will be based on the theory of these scales and categories but no two languages will necessarily have the same kind of linguistic material slotted in at any one point, though obviously there will be considerable overlap in many languages. The category of Unit, for example, is a theoretical category; it is represented in language by a stretch of language which carries grammatical patterns; wherever a grammatical choice is made, it is a unit which carries that choice. English happens to have five units (morpheme, word, group, clause and sentence) interrelated as demonstrated in Chapter 5. Other languages will have units but they may not be the same, either in number or kind, as in English. Again, Class is a theoretical category, which happens in English to be represented by such things as verb, noun (word classes) transitive or intransitive (clause classes) and so on. Other languages will have different **exponents** of the same categories. It is not possible to define the categories, for they are 'mutually defining'. As Halliday points out:

> Each of the four is specifically related to, and logically derived from, each of the others. There is no relation of precedence or logical priority among them. They are all mutually defining; as with theoretical categories in general, 'definition' in the lexicographical sense is impossible, since no one category

is defined until all the others are, in the totality of the theory.[1]

Terms such as 'group', 'clause', 'noun', 'verb' etc., belong to descriptive grammar, whereas the significance of scale and category is that it seeks to provide a theoretical basis on which to construct an adequate description. No description based on the theory has yet been fully formulated; much of the theory is still under discussion; the working out of any description based on the theory will inevitably be protracted. Elementary expositions of the functioning of, for instance, exponents of the category of unit such as is found in Chapter 5, can give some insight into grammatical patterning, but any general description of how 'English' works, is still some way off.

Unfortunately the publicity given to transformational-generative grammar (TG) in America, and more vaguely, to the 'new' grammar in this country has led to unwarranted expectations of something usable in every classroom appearing at any moment. Teachers in America have plunged in with considerable verve and considerable finance. In some areas of the country 'schoolroom TG' is a reality, though the findings of the linguists, on which teaching programmes have to be based, are not definitive, and constant revisions are inevitable. The fact that on the whole most English, or language teachers are not scientists, and have not been trained to think in terms of scientific theory, has perhaps made it difficult to appreciate the highly abstract nature of much current discussion about language, and has led to an expectation of practical results and applications at a stage earlier than is realistic or consistent with the nature of the theorising. As we have seen, theories of language are still in a state of flux, and descriptions of language based on these theories are incomplete both here and in other parts of the world. There is no basic dogma any longer; no longer can we trust in the comforting beliefs of orthodoxy. 'Old' grammars are discredited, the 'new' ones preached with fervour but also inevitably with the proviso that they are not yet complete; little of any 'new' grammar is yet accessible in the class-

1. M. A. K. Halliday, 'Categories of the Theory of Grammar' in *Word*, Vol. 17, No. 3.

rooms or even lecture halls in this country. It is an uncomfortable if stimulating period; as in sciences such as astronomy, we are only beginning to be aware of the extent of our ignorance. But one trend can perhaps be discerned in the linguistic world; the trend back to people, users of the language.

Traditional grammarians excluded people in so far as they could, in that while relying on their own 'educated intuition' they ignored the living force exerted by the great numbers of speakers of a language who willy-nilly changed the language almost out of recognition in a few centuries; structuralists ignored people in that they chose to ignore, to a greater or lesser degree, the meanings people attach to, or feel for language. But both in this country, and in America, linguists seem to be coming back, albeit from different directions, more directly to people, while psychologists and sociologists are in increasing numbers approaching people through their language. Many of the 'schools' of linguistics have indeed been influenced by the 'schools' of psychology. One of the great leaders of modern linguistics was Leonard Bloomfield, who was much influenced by 'behaviourism', a doctrine which considers the mind to be only an extension of the body, and which seeks to explain all human activity, including language, as a chain of material cause-effect sequences. Language was therefore explained by Bloomfield in terms of stimulus and response, and the inability to predict any specific utterance was thought to be the result only of an insufficient knowledge of the human nervous system, or of the influences upon it. In *Language* Bloomfield says, specifically:

We could foretell a person's actions (for instance whether a certain stimulus will lead him to speak, and, if so, the exact words he will utter), only if we knew the exact structure of his body at the moment, or, what comes to the same thing, if we knew the exact make-up of his organism at some early stage—say at birth or before—and then had a record of every change in that organism, including every stimulus that had ever affected the organism. The part of the human body responsible for this delicate and variable adjustment, is the nervous system . . .

127

Modern views of the central nervous system do not however support this view, and it is now more generally thought that the nervous system is made up of a number of hierarchical systems which are in some degree independent but which can and do interact in very complex ways which are not reducible to stimulus-response patterning. In addition, study of animal and human behaviour makes clear the existence of active creativity unrelated to any external stimulus, and of other behaviour patterns which seem determined by some factor other than response to a stimulus. It can be seen that transformational-generative grammar can accommodate the idea of creativity in that it lays down the rules permitting us to generate thousands of sentences never before heard and unrelated to any external pressure. Or again, is it coincidental that scale and category is based on the notion of a hierarchy of systems interacting and relating to each other? Scale and category is itself closely linked to the work of Firth and Malinowski, who, as linguist and anthropologist respectively, were very concerned with the interaction of language and society, and whose thinking on the 'context of situation' demanded the mutual study of language and its speakers.

It has been increasingly clear, in recent years, that many aspects of linguistic study relate closely to psychological theory, and conversely that, in order to discuss the psychology of child development in particular, and also some other aspects of psychology, an awareness of current linguistic theory is equally essential. A conference was held in 1965 in America on 'Language Development in Children', and the papers there presented and subsequently published as *The Genesis of Language* (edited Frank Smith and George A. Miller) did much to make clear the relationship of the two disciplines and to illustrate their mutual influence. At the same time, it has become clear how much is still unknown, and how much is still tentative. Both linguistics and psychology are disciplines which, over the last few years, have been questioning with great rigour some of the doctrines and assumptions of previous years, and it would be rash to assume that any of the work yet done in psycholinguistics is definitive.

9
The Conveying of Meaning

On page 12 it was pointed out that in order to understand how language worked, it would be necessary to chop it up in some rather arbitrary ways and to try to analyse it as a series of interrelating systems. It is now perhaps time to look at the various parts into which the previous chapters have dissected language and see how each contributes to an understanding of what language is and how it functions. Chapters 3 and 4 discussed sound systems, 5 looked at grammatical patterning, 6 looked at words and their relationship to non-linguistic facts, and 7 tried to show how any one language has in fact a number of other 'languages' within it, used for different purposes by different speakers on different occasions. The last chapter tried to show that any description of language will depend upon the basic theory about the nature of language which is adopted. Each of these chapters was fairly long, some of the subject matter rather difficult, even though only a very simplified summary of some aspects of language study, but all of them are necessary if incomplete contributions to the answering of the question as to how language succeeds in doing what is required of it.

Given a language event such as 'Good morning, John!', what is this event? To attempt to answer this fully, it would be necessary to consider the sounds, to distinguish the vowels and consonants and the intonation used; also to analyse the grammatical patterning of the greeting; the significance of each word, alone and in combination with the others would also need to be assessed, and the words would have to be placed in their social context. The implications, and possibly the results, of the choice of these three particular words rather than any others should also be considered. In order to collect this data, it would be necessary to decide beforehand what information was needed, and to work out how to relate all such scraps of information together and how to assess their relationship to each other and to the rest of the English language. That is, a language theory would have to be selected, in terms of which the material could be selected and ordered. This may sound an excessively complex way of describing a simple greeting, but if language is to be 'described', this is what has to be done. Language is very complex, more complex than even the crude procedures suggested above do justice to.

We are rarely aware of this complexity when we use our own language, although awareness of some aspects may come with the more difficult tasks such as, for instance, trying to pass an examination in English literature, compiling an involved report on a technical subject, or preparing an important television broadcast. But as soon as most of us set out to learn another language, or to analyse what is wrong with a foreigner's rendering of our native tongue, we begin to realise some of the difficulties. Schoolchildren and adults are often prepared to argue at length as to 'which is the most difficult language in the world', and rival claims are put forward for French as against German, Japanese as against Russian. But difficulties are only difficulties to those approaching a language analytically; to those who have spoken it since birth the language is not apparently difficult. Some of the practical results of realising this will be looked at in the next chapter.

It remains true, however, that for most of us, any language other than our own is 'difficult', and that the task of describing any language is 'difficult'. It is in fact impossible to describe 'Good morning, John!' simply; to attempt any description (other than a mere labelling as 'a greeting'), we have to take aspects such as sounds, grammar, context, etc., one at a time. Linguists call these different aspects **levels** and would say that language has to be described on a number of different levels.

As was pointed out earlier, language can be analysed in a number of different ways according to the use to which you want to put the analysis, and the identification of levels is no exception. Although there is considerable controversy among linguists over some of the finer points of distinction between levels, there is broad agreement over what are the main levels to be recognised. **Substance, form** and **context** are the names given to the main levels by Halliday, McIntosh and Strevens in *The Linguistic Sciences and Language Teaching,* and these are the ones we shall find it most convenient to look at here.

By substance is meant that part of language which is perceived by the senses—either sound heard, or symbols seen on the printed page. By form is meant the patterning of the various elements of language, and by context, the relation of these patterns to the rest of the world, i.e. to all events which are not themselves linguistic. The distinction of levels is obviously in one sense artificial, since all three levels operate simultaneously and overlap. But for the purposes of study each can be separated with a greater or lesser degree of clarity in relation to any particular language event. To study substance will of course be to study phonetics and phonology in the way outlined in Chapters 3 and 4; it will also imply the study of scripts and **graphology,** i.e. the various writing systems. The study of form will include the study of grammar, and of vocabulary (lexis), some approaches to which were suggested in earlier chapters. Finally, there is the study of context which concerns the relations between the language events and the rest of the world; this study is sometimes called **semantics** and concerns what the non-linguist generally has in mind when he talks about the meaning of an utterance. The terms semantics and meaning are often however used rather differently by linguists. Some linguists, moreover, deny that the study of meaning can legitimately be included in a study of linguistics—they prefer to exclude it, and regard it as a separate discipline.

Be that as it may, and there is no need to go into the arguments here, most of us who use and study language, are very deeply concerned with meaning in the way we understand the term. The fashionable concern with 'communication' referred to before, is a symptom of a deep and valid concern felt by many people at the lack of real understanding between people; the failure, as it seems, of language to convey meaning, and it is part of the intention of this book to give some perspective to the problems of communication by showing some of the complexities of language and its interpretation.

It seems appropriate here to turn to the point at which many textbooks of linguistics prefer to start—by looking at some definitions of language. One, which can be taken as fairly typical of many, is that offered by E. H. Sturtevant in *An Introduction to Linguistic Science*. He says that 'A language is a system of arbitrary vocal symbols by which members of a social group cooperate and interact'. A point which occurs in all such definitions needs stressing, namely the symbolic nature of language. Difficulties in communication often arise because this symbolic nature is overlooked. To many people the name of the thing, and the thing itself become identified—a (linguistic) 'table' *is* a table, a (linguistic) 'bicycle' *is* a bicycle. No great harm is done perhaps by such identification, though even here it is useful to point out that a (linguistic) 'table' is a generic term covering many varieties of table: wooden, metal, or papier mâché, high, low, four-legged or pedestal, square, round or oval, etc. But harm does result when linguistic items become equated with 'real world' items in cases where the equivalence is more ambiguous or vague, as when (linguistic) 'democracy' becomes equated with one particular system of government in one particular country at one particular time, or when (linguistic) 'truth' becomes equated with a personal view of a particular event. Words such as 'table', 'bicycle', 'democracy' and 'truth' are all only symbols and we cannot usefully discuss any of them without agreement as to the identity of what lies behind the symbol. One of the greatest dangers arises when a linguistic symbol which has acquired a pejorative connotation becomes identified with its **referent** (the thing to which it refers). Thus in varying parts of the world 'nigger' or 'whitey' have, linguistically, acquired emotional overtones of dislike, disgust or fear. If the symbol is identified with every possessor of a black skin or a white skin, as the case may be, then the emotional connotation is also transferred and it ceases to be possible to regard these human beings objectively. We accept and understand symbolism in some areas; we accept that a yellow line along the pavement symbolises a parking restriction, or that a red cross on a white background symbolises an organisation to help suffering, but we tend to ignore the symbolism of language, and to insist that truth lies in the saying of it.

'Then you should say what you mean,' the March Hare went on.

'I do,' Alice hastily replied, 'at least—at least I mean what I say—that's the same thing, you know!'

'Not the same thing a bit!' said the Hatter.

And Alice is far from being the only one to get her sayings and her meanings in some state of confusion. Her world and the Hatter's use their symbols differently:

Alice sighed wearily. 'I think you might do something better with the time,' she said, 'than waste it asking riddles with no answers.'

'If you knew Time as well as I do,' said the Hatter, 'you wouldn't talk about wasting *it*. It's *him*.'

'I don't know what you mean,' said Alice.

'Of course you don't!' the Hatter said, tossing his head contemptuously. 'I dare say you never even spoke to Time!'

'Perhaps not,' Alice cautiously replied, 'but I know I have to beat time when I learn music.'

'Ah! that accounts for it,' said the Hatter. 'He won't stand beating. Now if you only kept on good terms with him, he'd do almost anything you liked with the clock . . .'

And out of Wonderland, the confusion persists, because we use our symbols differently.

Because another thing people like the governor will never understand is that I *am* honest, that I've never been anything else but honest, and that I'll always be honest. Sounds funny. But it's true because I know what honest means according to me and he only knows what it means according to him. I think my honesty is the only sort in the world, and he thinks his is the only sort in the world as well.[1]

Sometimes, of course, symbols can be ambiguous, and the

1. Alan Sillitoe *The Loneliness of the Long Distance Runner*, W. H. Allen.

possible ambiguity can be, and is, deliberately exploited for various purposes. Ambiguity can, for instance, arrest attention in order to sell a product, as where a pun is used, for example in the advertisement for a well-known tobacco 'You deserve the good taste of GOLD LEAF. Why settle for less?' But sometimes ambiguity is used with less obvious intent, as when a product is advertised as 'available at the better stores'. Better than what? What does 'better' symbolise? Very little, perhaps, except a not-so-hidden appeal to English class consciousness.

The symbolism of trade names, or brand names, is an interesting study in itself. Sometimes a brand name comes to symbolise the whole range of similar products, as when 'Hoover' for many people, is still used to describe any type of suction operating cleaning machine, or as when 'Frigidaire' is used for all refrigerators. This was perhaps perpetuated by the little rhyme:

> *When Baby's cries grew hard to bear*
> *I popped him in the Frigidaire*
> *I never would have done so if*
> *I'd known that he'd be frozen stiff.*
> *My wife said 'George I'm so unhappé!*
> *Our darling's now completely frappé!*[1]

Advertisers do their best to achieve this sort of status for the words they contrive to describe products, and in the process of an advertiser creating a 'brand image' we can sometimes see the artificial process of a symbol creating 'reality', rather than the more usual route of symbol representing 'reality'.

The arbitrary nature of the symbols is seen in this process of word invention, and again, when languages are compared. A certain number of words in any one language may show a relation between their sound and what they represent, but a bell goes 'ding-dong' in English and 'bim-bam' in German. This not to deny the existence of onomatopoeic words, but to point out that they are few in number and only marginally related to non-linguistic phenomena. The now famous farmer who, leaning on the gate and observing his animals wallowing,

1. Harry Graham in the *Faber Book of Comic Verse*.

said 'Rightly is they called pigs' had not realised this and would no doubt have been discommoded to have it pointed out that some people called them 'Schweine', others 'cochons' and yet others 'nguruwe'. Perhaps he may have thought that 'others' had not such an 'expressive' language as he had. Other apparently less naïve speakers will also uphold the claims of a particular language to be more or less expressive, more or less clear, on grounds which are basically equally fragile. As has been pointed out before, language exists only through people, and is just as clear, expressive, logical or anything else as its speakers, over a period of time, want it to be. If genuine need is felt for new or different ways of expressing meaning, such ways will usually be found, though they may take time to achieve wide currency, or commonly accepted meaning.

The rest of the definition of language quoted on page 132 involves, in 'vocal', the recognition of the primacy of speech, dealt with in Chapter 2, and in the qualifying clause 'by which members of a social group co-operate and interact', a recognition of the view of the social nature of language. The use of 'system' in the definition is also to be noted; while the symbols of any one language may be arbitrary, they are not, in that language, arbitrarily used, but are used according to more-or-less fixed, more-or-less mutually agreed patterns. The degree of fixity and of agreement in the interpretation of the system is perhaps greatest on the level of grammar, for although there is great flexibility in the way in which grammatical patterns can be arranged and rearranged, there are limits within which the patterning has to be kept if the language is to remain comprehensible. The limits apply particularly to the question of ordering, at least in so far as the English language is concerned. Thus on the morphemic level it is not possible to alter the patterning of words with impunity; 'greenness' cannot become *'nessgreen', or 'talking' become *'ingtalk' without loss of intelligibility, and on the group level, it is not possible to say in English 'house the in' instead of 'in the house'. With a group such as 'the brick red house', intonation and meaning are substantially altered if the group is changed to 'the red brick house'. The degree of fixity and agreement on the semantic level is much less; the interpretation people put on the relationship between the sound or script to the actual world is much more fluid; to quote Alice, or rather Humpty Dumpty again, 'When I use a word ... it means just what I choose it to mean, neither more nor less'. On the level of phonology, it is probably safe to say that in English certain intonation patterns are fixed and obligatory, and few are ambiguous, unless deliberately made so, but individual vowel and consonant sounds have a range of acceptable variety permissible in so far as the system of distinctions between phonemes, the necessary contrasts, are not blurred.

To discuss the conveying of meaning, as the chapter heading suggests, is then to step into very deep waters, but in so far as a course can be charted, it may be seen that to understand how meaning is conveyed it is necessary to have an understanding of the different levels of language and their complex inter-relationship. We have to take into account the symbolic nature of language, with all that this implies by way of possible varying referents; we must consider the phonological and grammatical systems of patterning used by any one language and relate these patterns to the actual language event. We must also consider the relationship of the language form to the context. Above all, we must remember that the abstractions we make when study-ing language from a linguistic point of view are abstractions, and that since language is ultimately an attribute of people, the real study of meaning is a study of people. Likewise, in answer to the question 'What is Language?', we may use the definition quoted above, or something like it, but the definition is useful only as a shorthand reminder to the depths that lie below.

I 0

Language and Learning

The words 'language' and 'learning' in collocation would, for most people, signify the learning of a foreign language, for we rarely think of 'learning' our own language. Yet school time-tables are littered with periods labelled 'English', as well as with those labelled 'French' or 'German', and so perhaps it is necessary to distinguish between learning our own language and learning a foreign language and to see whether in fact one 'learns' one's own language, or whether it is acquired in a different way.

What is known about a child's acquisition of its mother tongue, and of learning to speak generally, is largely derived from the work of psychologists, who have sometimes employed tools offered by linguistic study, though not always with the accuracy or refinement which might be possible. A great deal is still unknown. The broad facts are observable, and apparently follow much the same pattern in all children regardless of the language of the parents. Briefly, the processes seem to be as follows.

The initial cry a baby makes as it is born is evidence that the lungs and larynx, organs necessary for life, and only incidentally for speech, are in working order, but apparently signifies little else. During the first few months of its life the baby makes a variety of different noises, such as crying or grunting; most of these are associated with bodily processes, and are probably mainly reflex actions. Soon, however, there are other sounds, generally referred to as 'babbling'. During this period, the sounds a baby makes tend at first to be vowel-like in quality, with consonant type sounds appearing only later. The sounds included in this 'babbling' cover a wide range, and are not necessarily restricted to the phonemes of any one language. They do not seem to be the result of any sort of imitation or mimicry on the child's part, but are apparently simply the result of the child's experimenting with its vocal organs and producing a variety of sounds without any discrimination.

Quite early on however, probably even before the end of the second month, the child begins to respond by movement, or other signs of attention, to the human voice. Some weeks later, these responses are differentiated so that response to a friendly tone of voice is apparently different from the response to a sharp or scolding voice. Before he is a year old, the child recognises certain specific words such as 'No', 'Walk', 'Dada', 'Drink' and so on, the particular selection depending now on his environment. Up to this stage his response to language is little more advanced than that of a trained animal, such as a dog, which has learnt to recognise certain words. In the second year however, he will usually start using some of these words himself with deliberate intent. The relationship between the earlier babbling, which uses all kind of phonemes, and the selection of certain phonemes when the child himself first uses sounds meaningfully is not entirely clear. The first meaningful sounds are apparently produced by imitation of an adult, but it seems as if the child, in order to imitate, has to learn these sounds, and does not select them from the sounds he already made in his babbling stages. According to Miller,[1] 'it is not uncommon to find that a child has produced / l / and / r / during its infantile babbling, but that later, at the age of two or three years, he is unable to produce these sounds correctly in English words ... He is not able spontaneously to use the phonetic elements of his babbling as the phonemes of his language.' The babbling, then, must be no more than preliminary muscular or physical activity.

Most psychologists recognise that somewhere around the age of two an important development takes place. To quote Vygotsky, 'At a certain moment at about the age of two, the curves of development, of thought and of speech, till then separate, meet and join to initiate a new form of behaviour.'[2] The child begins to realise, if dimly, the true function of speech and will

1. George Miller, *Language and Communication*. McGraw-Hill.
2. Vygotsky, *Thought and Language*. M.I.T.

actively try to master language. The further development of the relationship between thought and language has been, and is being increasingly explored, but must be more of a psychological than a linguistic study. From the age of about two, however, a child's mastery of language, given a normal social environment and normal ability, increases rapidly, and it has been shown that most children have, by the age of about six, mastered all the basic patterns of their language, and have acquired several thousand words (estimates of figures of vocabulary acquired vary considerably). From the age of about two, the child's language, while still derived partly from mimicry, becomes to an increasing extent independent of mimicry. It has been suggested that there are three processes involved in the child's acquisition of the basic patterns of the language, i.e. the skeleton of the syntax it requires. In the study published as 'A Child's Acquisition of Syntax' by Brown and Bellugi[1] these three processes are outlined. The first consists of imitation, though imitation is rarely exact or complete, but is usually 'reduced', i.e. certain words, mostly lexical words (see p. 68) are retained in the correct order, but grammatical words are frequently dropped. A second process consists of imitation of the child by the mother (or other adult) who expands an utterance a child has made by 'filling in' the grammatical words, and thereby teaching the child by first reinforcing what he has already learnt, and then taking him on beyond the limits of his own utterance. Examples quoted by Brown and Bellugi of the first process are, for instance:

Model Utterance:	*Child's imitation:*
'He's going out'	out'
'Fraser will be unhappy'	unhappy'

And of the second process:

Child:	*Mother:*
'Eve lunch'	'Eve is having lunch'
'Pick glove'	'Pick the glove up'

1. Ed. E. H. Lenneberg, *New Directions in the Study of Language.* M.I.T.

A third process is more recognisably creative on the part of the child. If a child produces a 'correct' utterance, it is difficult to say for sure whether it is an imitation of something heard, even if not immediately beforehand, or whether it is something he has spontaneously produced. If however he produces something like the example quoted in Brown and Bellugi:—'I digged a hole', we can be pretty sure he is creating a bit of speech, and we can also see that he is creating it on the basis of a stock of words and a fixed pattern, an 'internal grammar', so as to speak, which gives him correct word order, correct person and number for the pronoun, and correct association of indefinite article and noun, but which does not yet extend to the correct tense form of the verb. A similar example quoted by another writer is when a six-year-old child asked him to 'higher the swing' (cf. 'lower the swing'), and most of us can recall similar childish 'mistakes'.

There is room for controversy over the adequacy or completeness of these particular findings. Work in this field is difficult, as is illustrated by the authors' anecdote:

> 'Adam,' we asked, 'which is right, "two shoes" or "two shoe"?' His answer on that occasion, produced with explosive enthusiasm, was 'Pop goes the weasel!' The two-year-old child does not make a perfectly docile experimental subject.

But it seems incontestable that the acquisition of most grammatical patterns comes relatively early in the child's life, without any conscious teaching or learning of grammar as such. Has he then 'learned' English by the age of about six? Is there anything left other than to extend vocabulary and to acquire a few more complicated structures? A great deal, of course remains, but there is not always unanimity on what it is that is left.

Language is sometimes spoken of as a skill, or set of skills, and learning it is said to be more like learning to ride a bicycle than learning quadratic equations or the names of the Kings of England. It may be true that a child acquires his native language in a way somewhat analogous to the learning of other skills, though the comparison would seem to be a facile and dangerous one, and it is especially mischievous if it leads anyone to think of the end products as having much in common. The skill of riding a bicycle is, for anyone other than a circus performer, virtually complete once the wheels have revolved a few times while the feet are on the pedals, but the mastery of language is only beginning with the acquisition of basic syntax and a few words. English in schools is devoted, one way or another, to the development of basic skills into something which is likely to have a bearing on the whole of a child's life. In so far as primary schools are concerned, there has been, as the Plowden report made clear, something of a revolution in the attitude to language. 'English' will perhaps rarely appear on the timetable, for there is increasingly greater flexibility in the curriculum and the younger the child the less marked are the divisions between subjects. Even the three R's may now perhaps not be timetabled as such, for once the very early stages are past, reading, writing and arithmetic may be taught together with history and geography in the course of making a study of fishing, or of bridges, or of timber, or of any one of a number of other possible 'centres of interest'. But also, in the primary school, there is likely to be time set aside for stories, for the use of language in the imaginative interpretation through language of life. The Plowden report comments on the use of stories in schools:

> We are convinced of the value of stories for children, stories told to them, stories read to them and the stories they read for themselves. It is through story as well as through drama and other forms of creative work that children grope for the meaning of the experiences that have already overtaken them, savour again their pleasure and reconcile themselves to their own inconsistencies and those of others.

Often English, Drama and Poetry are seen as one and the same subject, and junior school children will be encouraged to use their own language to act out, or write about, both direct personal experience and imaginatively acquired experience. To quote Plowden again: 'Experience and language interact all the time: words come to life in the setting of sensory experience and vivid imaginative experience.' In many, though perhaps

141

not yet all, primary schools then, teachers try to foster the emotional, social and intellectual growth of the child by encouraging him to use language as freely and fluently as possible. In such schools, there is likely to be also increasing realisation of the importance of speech, of the spoken word, in sharp distinction to the older days of the silent classroom, the bowed heads and the diligent scratching of pens. It is perhaps true to say that whereas language once tended to be taught as an end in itself, it is now seen much more as an instrument of personal and mental growth.

Later in school life, however, the pattern of 'English' is on the whole less revolutionary. English teachers in secondary schools can perhaps be roughly divided into those who see their main aim as being to develop in their pupils a sensitivity to, and aesthetic appreciation of, the best in English literature, those who see their main task as being to give their pupils the ability to write clear and 'correct' English, and a smaller number, perhaps who see English as 'the true education of the life-flame', to quote David Holbrook.[1]

Some of course would say that, by doing the first two you achieve the third; others would claim that by aiming at the third you probably achieve the first two, and no one, probably, would be prepared to discount the value of any of these aims, but would regard them as complementary. Perhaps it would be fairer to sort out the teachers not by aims, but by methods. Thus some concentrate on the intensive and detailed scrutiny of various 'classic' works of literature; others on the writing of exercises, essays, reports, summaries and so on, and yet others on the self-expression to be found in what is often called 'creative' writing. In some schools the greater flexibility between subjects noted in the primary schools is encouraged in at least the earlier stages of secondary education, so that English teaching may be only part of a much broader area of the curriculum. In these circumstances, language work is likely to be seen as integral to everything that is done in school. But perhaps most teachers, and most schools, move around these different approaches from time to time, uneasily or perhaps easily, trying

1. *Spectator* 14th October, 1960.

one and then the other according to personal inclination, the demands of a specific examination or the requirements of a departmental syllabus.

Some, but perhaps increasingly few, spend timetable periods on the analysis and parsing of sentences and the formal study of English grammar. Professor R. Quirk, however, amongst others, has said that he

> ... doubted the value of any kind of grammar teaching for improving written performance. There was a sharp difference between foreign language teaching (where one certainly had to learn grammar before being able to use the language) and the teaching of English, the mother-tongue (where all the grammar had been learnt before the teaching began). The teaching of mother-tongue grammar on the lines of 'foreign-language grammar' was assumed to lead to a better command of the mother-tongue. This was an unproven, and to many teachers a dubious assumption; it wasted time, frustrated teachers, and prevented the development of an educationally more valuable kind of English teaching.[1]

Views such as this have been gaining considerable acceptance in recent years, although still hotly disputed by some. But even those who accept such opinions often feel vaguely uneasy at not putting something else in the place of traditional grammar.

While the problem of what 'English' teaching is, or should be, cannot easily be solved—like most complicated problems there is no single or easy answer—yet perhaps it can be put into some perspective. The pivot around which all these approaches to 'English' revolve is quite simply and obviously 'language'. In all its different ways, English teaching is language teaching first and foremost, that is, it is the teaching of the use and significance of systems and sets of symbols. As we saw earlier, these symbols are arbitrary and often ambiguous. For a further example, compare the use of the symbol 'truth' in the following:

1. From talk 'On Conceptions of Good Grammar' given as Giff Edmonds Memorial Lecture for the Royal Society of Literature on 15th June, 1967. Quoted in *Times Educational Supplement* of 23rd June, 1967.

> *(a) Beauty is truth, truth beauty—that is all*
> *Ye know on earth and all ye need to know.*

> *(b) Her terrible tale*
> *You can't assail*
> *With truth it quite agrees.*
> *Her taste exact*
> *For faultless fact*
> *Amounts to a disease.*

It is no simple process that teaches a child to disentangle the widely different 'realities' behind the single symbol 'truth' and which also enables him to relate both these 'realities' to some inner reality of his own. At the age of four, five or six the child will almost certainly have heard the word: 'Tell the *truth*, Johnnie!', though it is by no means certain that he and his mother interpret it in the same way, but a great deal has to happen to that child before he uses it, or recognises it, as used in (*b*), and much more still before (*a*) has any significance to him. If it is difficult to analyse the way in which a child acquires his syntax, it is even more difficult to analyse the way in which he acquires his knowledge of linguistic symbolism. Both are perhaps essentially related to a process of growth, rather than to a process of accumulation of data. Such studies as have been made of the development of language and the child usually stop short at pre-secondary age, but it is perhaps reasonable to think that language development might proceed along similar lines until considerably later. Even so, the processes are still far from adequately known. In a paper on 'The Early Growth of Language Capacity in the Individual', Leonard Carmichael refers to the evidence linking the physical development of the brain with the stages of 'speech readiness', and says that, 'in the postnatal life of the infant certain centers of the brain of the growing infant must reach a specific level of development before the learning of linguistic patterns that are "meaningful" is possible. This level of brain capacity must emerge before the child begins to learn the linguistic forms that are typical of the social group in which it is reared.' One can only, as a layman, speculate whether the capacity for extended uses of linguistic symbolism is also related in some way to that growth which goes on for many years beyond infancy, and beyond the six-year-old stage at which the child has mastered so many basic patterns. It would not seem an unreasonable hypothesis in view of the fact that at birth the human brain is only 23 per cent of its final size, that it grows rapidly for the next six years, and that the whole growing process of the brain is not complete until about ten years after sexual maturity, i.e. until about the twenty-third year of life. What does seem clear, from other evidence, however, is that children tend to do much better, educationally, when there is no sharp break or division between the language of the home and the language of the school, so that language 'growth' as it were, can be continuous rather than discontinuous.

In an earlier chapter discussing varieties of language, it was pointed out that certain registers are considered more appropriate than others for specific purposes, and also that it has been suggested that some children are thought to have access to fewer linguistic codes than others, with it is thought, detrimental effect on their ability to profit by the present educational system. What in fact happens is that children from some homes find that when they come to school, they have, as it were, to learn a new language, whereas children from other homes find little or no discrepancy between the language of the home and the language of the school. In the first case, growth may be interrupted or diverted into different channels, in the second, growth can be continuous and therefore more effective.

Whether these hypotheses are accepted or not, it is surely fair to suggest that for all children 'English' teaching should have as its central aim, the nurturing of a process of growth that gives the child the necessary linguistic resources to handle the increasingly difficult tasks involved, as he goes through school life, not only in the educational processes, but also in the total emotional and intellectual demands made on him. Such educational processes will, for instance, demand that he masters complex conceptual material of a high degree of abstraction, and will also demand that he should be aware of, and able to

145

select appropriately from the resources of the mother tongue those elements which will best suit particular and specialised purposes. Or the emotional and intellectual demands on him may, for example, require degrees of introspection and analysis difficult to achieve without adequate language. It should be clear that 'English' teaching alone cannot teach him to think. The relationship between language and thought is still far from clear, but it is unlikely, to say the least, that language alone leads to concept formation. Without adequate linguistic resources, however, thinking is often made much more difficult. Again, the selection of appropriate language forms implies a mastery of a wide range of linguistic resources, but also other qualities of discrimination and judgement not necessarily wholly attributable to language mastery.

To master a wide range of language forms implies, however, that the registers of literature are not necessarily the only, or even in all circumstances, the best, registers on which to concentrate study. In so far as the study of literature is the study of life, and of people, there is no need to justify it, for its value is self-evident. But the study of literature is only too often still narrowly interpreted in schools, and it becomes a stereotyped discipline along with other factual subjects, so that one 'learns' Shakespeare in the same way as one 'learns' the River Amazon, or perhaps with even less excitement. Where such a view of literature is taken, it may exclude the creation of the child's own literature, or may deny him the opportunity of looking at uses of language other than the purely literary. But even where literature is meaningfully taught, there is surely also a case for making children aware of those uses of language which have nothing to do with literature, but which pervade much of their lives—the insidious language of advertising, the seemingly omniscient language of the half-truths of much journalism, the glib and honeyed language of the women's magazines, the glib and tough language of screen warfare and conflict. Teachers often seem to suppose that, by some alchemy of the mind, good literature drives out bad, but the supposition is dubious. For most of us, it is only by awareness of the many different uses of language that effective discrimination, and

146

effective communication, can be achieved with any degree of certainty.

How precisely, if at all, the study of linguistics can be helpful in defining the role of English teaching and learning cannot yet be codified. Much work is being done in this field in the U.S.A., and in this country, the Nuffield Programme in Linguistics and English Teaching at the Communication Research Centre at University College, London will no doubt be fruitful. But perhaps a linguist's view of language can offer some pointers. The linguist's recognition of speech as the primary language form, contrasts with the sometimes entrenched view of the supremacy of the written word, particularly if it is a 'classic' written word. The recognition of the complex relationship between speech and writing may be of interest. The perspective given to 'correctness' and to language change, and the historical view of language can perhaps modify some of the more rigid and prescriptive approaches. The realisation that ability may be masked if linguistic resources to match the ability are not available; an appreciation of the nature of meaning as something other than a dictionary definition and a few idioms; all these may be found eventually to be not teaching points but necessary areas of awareness for the teacher. But most valuable of all perhaps will be the closer linking of language with society, or better, with people.[1] A detached and critical study of at least some of the various registers and codes of a language, and an awareness of the social implications of the choices which everyone constantly has to make in using language, could surely be of benefit to teachers. In so far as the study of literature is concerned, the tools offered by linguistic analysis can perhaps be of use, not only to higher criticism, but also to less advanced students trying to see how a writer can achieve the effects he needs.

---

1. One begins to suspect that the linguistic symbol 'society' is undergoing a metamorphosis. It seems to be so often now used for something impersonal which involves everyone else except the speaker. Thus on a television broadcast recently, in a discussion concerning the moral obligations of scientific research workers, the scientists in the programme repeatedly affirmed 'It is not *our* responsibility—it is society's responsibility to decide how to use the products of our research'—as though society was something apart from them, something to which they did not belong.

Linguistic analysis will however, be only one more means of approach to literary criticism, and is not to be confused with criticism itself.

No mention has yet been made of the area in which teachers tend to expect most of the linguists—namely in the provision of a 'new grammar'. It should be clear from much of what has been said earlier in the book that linguists are not concerned with prescriptive grammars, i.e. with sets of rules laying down 'correct' forms of language use. They are, however, very concerned with descriptive grammars, that is, with analyses of languages as they are used and according to the various kinds of patterning—the various levels. Few, if any, languages can yet boast of having any such adequate descriptive grammar available. But work is continuing, and partial descriptions, descriptions of one or more aspects, gradually appear, are contested, modified, rewritten and reappear. In short, there is as yet no 'new grammar', though there is a good deal of new thinking about grammar, some small part of which was outlined in an earlier chapter.

But although there is no 'new grammar' much of the thinking behind it has percolated into the teaching of foreign languages, both here and abroad, and it is in this field that linguistic views of language have come nearest to general acceptance and use, even though in some places foreign language teaching regrettably remains unaffected by them. The acceptance of some of this thinking has coincided with the widespread development of technological aids to such teaching, and it is unfortunate that where the use of such aids, or the methods used in conjunction with them, have sometimes been illjudged, the linguists have tended to come under fire at the same time, and their work to be confused with some of the misuses, by others, of that work. Some of the methods of teaching foreign languages which are now most widely popular are often referred to as 'audio-lingual' methods. These methods are based originally on a number of assumptions about language. Some of these assumptions were in turned based on the work of certain psychologists, notably B. F. Skinner. Chief among these was the assumption that foreign language learning is, like certain other kinds of learning, basically a question of habit formation, and therefore largely mechanical. The more extreme proponents of such views therefore believed that language could be taught by endless repetitions of certain patterns of language, patterns which could be provided by the structural linguists. These patterns would be learned by administering certain verbal stimuli and expecting certain specific verbal responses. This was obviously a task well adaptable to the use of technological aids such as tape recorders and language laboratories, and the result was too often a series of dull and repetitive drills, often administered wholly via machines, and with only occasional intervention by the teacher. But common sense, as well as the spread of different kinds of theories, has tended to modify this approach. Chomsky, whose work was mentioned in an earlier chapter, made a vigorous attack on Skinner's theories of verbal behaviour, and the work of other linguists and psycholinguists has recently been more concerned to look for different explanations for the ability to produce language. The theories of 'competence' and 'performance' (p. 123) are of course particularly relevant. Some interesting research is being conducted, using the transformational-generative approach, on such things as the language abilities of ESN children, and on other related topics.

Modern foreign language teaching techniques tend therefore to recognize the element of habit formation at the earlier stages of language learning, but make only limited use of mere stimulus-response situations. Such modern techniques are based on the belief that foreign languages are best taught through active speech, taught in a carefully selected and graded progression of structures, but always set in as realistic a situation as possible. Such a method is a combination of the **oral, structural** and **situational approaches.** Up until recently the method most widely favoured—in fact it was often considered to be the only method—of teaching a foreign language was what is now often referred to as the **grammar-translation** method. This is too well known to need much description. Children taught in this way usually learnt the 'rules' of the grammar, including numbers of paradigms, and had to translate into and from written forms of the foreign language. Oral work may have played a minor role, being allotted say, 10 per cent or less marks in some terminal examination, and attention paid to it would reflect this proportion. Material for translation usually came from a very restricted range of registers, the bulk of it most probably being of a literary nature. In modern teaching, such translation is likely to come at some point much nearer the end of the course, it at all, and instruction in translation is likely to be regarded as a separate activity from that of learning to use the language creatively.

By the oral approach (or more accurately the aural-oral approach) is meant that these skills are taught first—listening, then speaking. Reading and writing in the foreign language come later, often considerably later. It will be seen that this accords with the linguist's idea of the primacy of speech, and the realisation that speech has techniques such as intonation and rhythm which can be only crudely, if at all, transferred to writing. To this extent speech is a more complete expression of language than writing. Anyone who can speak a language fluently will have less trouble, it is believed, in learning to read and write it, than will a person who has to learn to speak a language which he has first mastered in print only. Evidence to support this belief is not conclusive, and more research needs to be done; meanwhile many teachers believe it is sound. It also, of course, accords with the way in which the mother tongue is learnt, where speech certainly comes before writing, and many people will say that the nearer foreign language teaching can approach to the way in which the mother tongue is acquired, the more effective it is likely to be.

The structural approach means that the patterns of the language are carefully analysed, selected and graded, and are then taught methodically. To some extent of course, as will be realised, this is a counsel of perfection if not of impossibility. To analyse, select and grade the structures of a language pre-supposes an adequate description of that language, and as we have seen, this is not yet available in full measure for any language. Nevertheless, it has not been found necessary to await such full description. Inventories of, for instance, English sentence patterns for the purpose of teaching English abroad were made as early as 1934 by Palmer, and more recently by Fries and Hornby. The basic sentence types set out by Paul Roberts and quoted on pages 83–84 have been made the basis of English teaching method, although in this case for native speakers. Most of the modern language courses now produced, including audio-visual or audio-lingual courses, claim to use 'graded structures', although the principles on which the grading is done may be very different from one course to another. But they have in common the approach which selects, on some basis, a particular grammatical pattern—a 'structure' —which is then presented, and drilled, until the learner is thought to have absorbed the pattern. Ideally, the teacher then 'exploits' this material, and the learner is encouraged to use the pattern in a number of other ways. Where this exploitation is inadequate, of course, the drilling is liable to lead to parrot-like repetition and stereotyped responses, and the learner may be unable to utilise or adapt the pattern to other situations. But a good teacher, with an informed knowledge of language and how it works, will be able to select, grade, drill and exploit such structures as seem most appropriate to his pupils' needs, especially in the earlier stages of language learning.

'His pupils' needs'—this lies at the heart of the third approach —that based on situation. Much foreign language teaching, at least in this country, has in the past been concerned only with the language of literature. There are many reasons why this should be changing; the war gave a great impetus to the learning of other languages for practical purposes; people travel more freely and feel the need for a mastery of language in registers other than the literary; businessmen are increasingly conscious of the need for what might be called 'day-to-day' language. The tremendous growth that has taken place in the teaching of English abroad, where the status of English as a world language has stimulated demand for the teaching of English for a variety of purposes, has also been very influential in its effects on language teaching at home. In many of these situations, 'literary' language was found to be inadequate, and the language taught had to be related to the precise needs of the scholar, soldier, traveller or businessman. Courses in specific registers of a language did of course exist in the past, as for example, 'German for Scientists' or 'French for Businessmen' and so on, but in the main, the concessions to the needs that such courses made were largely at the level of vocabulary, and scientifically based courses for specific purposes, and including an adequate oral component, were, and still are, rare. Nevertheless the emphasis is changing, and particularly in the more elementary courses, much more effort now tends to be made towards teaching in a way which recognises language in its social perspective. But although 'The pen of my aunt' may be a linguistic chestnut, it is far from dead. A book published in the last few years, in a series which is often good, includes in one volume where a widely used European language is presented for self-teaching, the following sentences: 'He died of gout,' in the same exercise as 'He has translated this book from the German while he was staying with his aunt.' An earlier exercise includes in immediate proximity the sentences: 'The cow is not brown,' 'Is the nut ripe?', 'Is the night not dark?', and 'Is the sausage ready?' Anyone learning the foreign language equivalents of these sentences could obviously only learn them by rote, and not in any meaningful way. Even a highly experienced teacher might find it hard to devise a situation for teaching purposes which includes these sentences all at one time.

'To devise a situation.' So far, I have been talking about the learner's situation and his needs. Most people would accept that it is quite impossible to learn the whole of any language, for even in our native tongue there are many technical things we cannot readily talk or write about. Perhaps it will also be accepted that if one can only teach part of a language one should teach that part which is most relevant to the learner's needs at a particular stage; that one should, for instance, teach him the language necessary to find his way to the Louvre before one teaches him the language of art criticism, or that he should learn to be able to buy bread and cheese before being able to take part in a discussion on manufacturing processes. Sometimes of course, it is just possible that the needs of the learner may dictate 'dying of gout' before 'buying bread and cheese', but these would be unusual and highly specific needs. Language teaching is then, to be related to the situation of the learner. But this is not what teachers always mean when they talk of a 'situational approach'.

They are as likely to be referring to a method of teaching, a way of conveying the meaning of a foreign language. As has been seen in an earlier chapter, the question of meaning is very complicated, and to teach anyone a meaning in a language other than his own may well be difficult. To solve the problem, a teacher may use one or more of a number of different methods. He may explain in the native tongue, or he may translate into the native tongue. Apart from grave theoretical objections to these methods, they may lead to difficulties on occasion, as when words or phrases have to be dealt with for which there is no exact equivalent in the other language. Such words might be 'the' or 'quite' or even lexical words like 'home', none of which may be directly translatable into another language, and which may give difficulty in explanation. Alternatively, in order to teach meaning, a teacher may use **ostensive** methods, i.e. he attempts to teach meaning through sensual perception. He will point to, and name, objects such as tables and chairs, or contrast objects, or qualities of objects or people, (short and tall children, for instance), or he may teach prepositions by actually moving objects from 'in' to 'on' or 'over' some other object. Again gestures and actions may be used to demonstrate meaning, the teacher announcing what he is doing at the moment of doing it. In due course the learners will take over the actions and gestures and will themselves use the appropriate language at the same time. They will then be using language while themselves participating in the appropriate activity. The aim of the teacher is to put the language which is to be learnt into a context so that the learner may live the language or may experience the situation and the language that accompanies that situation.

It is obvious that classroom conditions impose a strict limit on this sort of living language situation, but in the belief that the method is one of the most efficient ways of conveying meaning, the teacher then seeks to devise situations where, even if inevitably in a somewhat artificial way, the learner may

F

experience and use language in a fully contextualised way. Ways of devising situations may vary from the presentation of pictures, models or films to the acting out of a play. If, for instance one wishes to teach 'sun' on a day when clouds lour over the classroom, one may devise a sunny situation with the help of a picture of the sun. Or winter can be taught in the middle of summer by means of appropriate pictures. Film strips, slides and ciné films can give the illusion of situations remote from the classroom. But in all cases the teaching aim is the same: to present appropriate language to a learner who can either be or, with a little effort, can imagine himself to be, in a living situation.

It will be obvious of course that the three approaches outlined—oral, structural and situational, have their limitations when it comes to more advanced levels of language learning. At some point the learner may have to concentrate on written texts; sooner or later structural exercises will be valuable only for remedial work in areas where he has difficulty, and there is a limit to the extent to which even the most resourceful teacher can devise situations. But there is little doubt that for the earlier and intermediate stages of language teaching, these methods can be stimulating and effective. Even here, though, structural drills can have their danger; they can be used to produce only stereotyped responses to stereotyped situations, and excessive reliance on this sort of work can be as sterile and futile as was much of the learning of paradigms, conjugations and so on in earlier periods. The teacher has always to remember that language is essentially creative and must foster the ability of the learner to create as well as to respond. In the advanced stages, the problems become more like those of advanced mother tongue learning, and may be susceptible of similar treatment. Even at more advanced levels, however, the learner will lack language experience in the foreign tongue in many areas where he is well experienced in the mother tongue, and efforts will have to be made to enable him to 'catch up' in these areas.

These then are perhaps some of the ways in which linguistic thinking has affected language teaching methods. But there is another area in which linguistics has had an effect, though one whose value may be controversial, and which is certainly not fully developed. This is in the field known as **contrastive** linguistics.

As with much else, there is nothing very new in this except in the realisation of the extent and thoroughness to which it can be carried. Most language teachers in the classroom have at one time or another used as a teaching point the differences between the mother tongue and the language they are teaching: 'In English, the adjective comes before the noun, but in French it usually, though not always, comes after it', or: 'In French, the tongue must be higher in the mouth for the / i / sound in "lit" than it is for the English / i / in "see",' and so on. Contrastive linguistic analysis seeks to make it possible to extend such statements by studying two languages in detail and selecting for contrast those areas where differences are apparent. Semantic and lexical differences can, in theory, be analysed, but until adequate studies are made of languages in these fields contrast is difficult, though some statements can be made. In general, much more progress has been made with phonetic and structural than with lexical and semantic studies and contrastive linguistic studies have in the main therefore concentrated on these areas.

The chapter on 'The Sounds of Language' showed how English and French vowels could usefully be contrasted by means of the Cardinal vowel system. While it would be unwise to teach beginners, especially children, by any academic exercises based on such charts, it is very useful for the teacher to be able to draw on such contrastive studies and to be himself aware of the areas of possible difficulty. Thus while it may be obvious that English, in contrast to French, has no nasalised vowels, the precise difference between somewhat similar vowels in the two languages may be elusive without analysis and contrast of each. Similarly with consonants: / t / and / d / in French are not quite the same as / t / and / d / in English; French and English / r / are clearly and audibly different, but different in what way? Is / l / always the same in both languages? A phonetic analysis and contrast of the sound systems of both languages will provide answers to these questions, and therefore a sound basis for teaching, though not necessarily, it must be repeated, a set of teaching points. Young learners especially, are likely to do better by attempting to mimic rather than by being taught analytically, but the teacher will be enabled to select and grade areas for teaching on the basis of his knowledge of the contrasts.

Most laymen have no difficulty in recognising that no two languages sound the same. Even when one cannot distinguish the words of an utterance, it is normally possible and easy to say whether the speaker is speaking our own tongue, or a foreign tongue—everything except English sounds 'funny' to an Englishman, including a foreigner's pronunciation of English, and unfamiliar English dialects. But it is often less easy to understand that different languages have different grammatical categories. For centuries grammarians in all parts of the world have tried to find elements of grammar that could be applied to any language, but the search has been unrewarding. It is doubtful if it is even safe to say that every language has something like nouns, and something like verbs. In the account of scale and category grammar in Chapter 8 you will remember that the categories of class, unit, structure and system were said to be universal, but these are highly abstract categories, whose exponents will vary in every language. Each language has its own grammar, which will be like the grammar of related languages in some ways, but unlike them in others. In the next chapter we will see how languages are related to each other; the closer the relationship the more likenesses we may find, but no languages have identical grammatical structures. In teaching another language, it is therefore useful to be aware of those areas of similarity and dissimilarity of structure in order to identify points of possible difficulty. For instance the English and French sentences:

(*a*) The book is on the table
(*b*) Le livre est sur la table

show essentially the same structure, but a sentence with the same meaning in say, Swahili:

(*c*) Kitabu kiko mezani

obviously has a very different structure—observable even to anyone knowing no Swahili from the fact that the same meaning is apparently conveyed in three rather than in six words. Contrastive analysis is also likely to point out those structures which have no equivalent in the native tongue, and which therefore need special teaching. An example might be the German imperative form:

(*d*) Komm du doch mit!

which exists in addition to the other type of imperative:

(*e*) Komm!

which has a near counterpart in English 'Come!' while (*d*) has no structural equivalent in English.

While some textbooks make tacit or even overt use of contrastive analysis, there are as yet only a few texts available which set out directly to provide contrastive analysis between any two languages. The very useful and extensive bibliography in W. F. Mackey's *Language Teaching Analysis* includes a list, many of which however are relatively brief treatments of small areas.

Semantic contrasts are, as has been suggested, much more difficult both to analyse and describe, but one cannot learn a new language for very long without being aware of their importance. The difficulty arises partly out of the different denotative range, connotations, associations and semantic fields of various words in different languages. For example, Swahili 'ndugu' has a far wider denotative range than any one word in English, for the *Swahili–English Dictionary* shows it can mean: 'brother, sister, cousin, relation, fellow-tribesman (citizen, countryman)'. Again, in English 'cousin' covers male and female cousins, whereas many languages will require different words for female and male cousins. Connotations vary widely between different languages; words may be inter-translatable, but may not convey the same meaning, as with 'mzee' in Swahili, which is literally, 'an old person', but which also has connotations of respect, authority and dignity which do not necessarily attach to 'an old person' in English.

With this latter point however, we begin to move into the

range not only of linguistic contrast, but of cultural contrast. The connotations of 'mzee' in Swahili are different from the connotations of 'old person' in English because old people are, or at any rate until recently were, regarded differently in the different cultures. Such cultural differences in word meaning have been referred to earlier, in Chapter 6, where it was pointed out that even as between British and American English there were differences in connotation of the same word, arising out of contrasting cultural influences. 'A smart youngster' may be approved of in the U.S.A., but is there not a slightly pejorative ring to 'smart' in this country?

Many teachers prefer to avoid direct reference to contrasts between the mother tongue and the foreign language being learned. They believe that a language is best learned in and through itself, again rather as one learns the mother tongue, only a small part of which is ever learnt by definition or analysis by the native speaker. It would seem to be useful however, if teachers were aware of areas of contrast, whether phonological, structural, semantic or cultural, in order that special care can be paid to points of potential difficulty, and accurate analysis of the reasons for particular errors made.

Much learning of language—one's own or even a foreign language, is apparently intuitive; it is only an exceptionally gifted teacher who can afford to teach intuitively. 'Intuition' and 'sensibility' are words much used in discussion on the teaching or learning of English in schools today, but neither of them are terms which can bear very close inspection in the context of teaching. Too often 'intuition' is thought of as something almost magical, rather like a sixth sense, but like the sixth sense, it is often reducible to a particularly skilled and rapid collation of information from other senses, combined with certain analytical (but unanalysed) mental processes. In order to develop an apparently intuitive mastery of language, the learner must be subjected to many different linguistic experiences. With a child learning his native tongue the quality of linguistic experience in his home background is likely to decide, more than any other factor, the quality of his mastery of language, for this is where he has experienced it most—day in and

day out over all the years of his infancy and childhood. In order
to teach language in circumstances where these years of linguistic experience cannot, in the nature of things, be replicated,
the teacher cannot afford to rely on his own or his pupils'
'intuition' but has to make an analysis of particular linguistic
requirements and see that teaching methods are designed to
provide means whereby these requirements can be met as
economically and efficiently as possible. The child need not,
indeed it is better that he does not, at least in the early stages,
analyse language; it is essential that the teacher does. At the
later stages of learning, and for adult pupils, it is probable that
an analytical approach, complementary to other approaches,
will help rather than hinder language mastery, particularly
where the learning of foreign languages is concerned. Indeed
more intelligent children will often be found to demand analytic
reasons for certain facets of language, even in the early stages,
and it is usually wrong to withhold analytic methods of approach, either to the learning of a foreign language, or to
increasing mastery of one's own native tongue, in cases where
such an approach is either demanded or otherwise seems appropriate. A good teacher has a variety of tools, and a good learner
learns in a variety of different ways.

Learning our own language, learning foreign languages; in
both of these language is obviously the main centre of interest.
But language is pervasive throughout education; a great deal
of what we learn is in some degree or other the learning of
language. Perhaps we can paint, compose or play music, handle
a saw or a screwdriver, knit, sew or cook without language,
though it is difficult to envisage anyone going much beyond the
elementary levels of performance in these activities without
some command of language. When it comes to geography,
physics, history, economics, or any other such field of study, to
do without language is inconceivable. In all such studies we
have to learn language, although language is not here the centre
of interest. Often its role in the learning process is taken for
granted, and mastery of the specific registers required has to be
as it were 'absorbed through the skin' rather than being accorded any planning or consideration.

Language and Linguistics

In the more specifically language subjects—English and the foreign languages—concentration on the mechanics of language is sometimes allowed to blur the true functions of language; in the subjects which are not primarily language subjects, the mechanics of language are sometimes ignored. It is perhaps the most important task of the language teacher to try to modify both attitudes—to encourage realisation of the true nature and functions of language as an integral part of human life and society, and also to enable students to acquire the linguistic resources necessary to equip them to cope adequately with the tasks with which they are likely to be confronted. Language and learning are indivisible.

I I

Language Past and Present

As has been seen earlier, it is very difficult to represent speech forms in writing, but look at the following examples of written representations of colloquial speech:

(*a*)

MERCUTIO: Thou art like one of those fellows that, when he enters the confines of a tavern, claps me his sword upon the table, and says, 'God send me no need of thee!' and, by the operation of the second cup, draws it on the drawer, when, indeed, there is no need.

BENVOLIO: Am I like such a fellow?

MERCUTIO: Come, come, thou art as hot a Jack in thy mood as any in Italy; and as soon moved to be moody, and as soon moody to be moved.

BENVOLIO: An what to?

MERCUTIO: Nay, and there were two such, we should have none shortly, for one would kill the other. Thou! why, thou wilt quarrel with a man that hath a hair more or a hair less in his beard than thou hast; thou wilt quarrel with a man for cracking nuts, having no reason but because thou hast hazel eyes;—what eye, but such an eye, would spy out such a quarrel? Thy head is as full of quarrels as an egg is full of meat; and yet thy head hath been beaten as addle as an egg for quarrelling; thou hast quarrell'd with a man for coughing in the street, because he hath waken'd thy dog that hath lain asleep in the sun; didst thou not fall out with a tailor for wearing his new doublet before Easter? with another, for tying his new shoes with old riband? and yet thou wilt tutor me from quarrelling!

BENVOLIO: An I were so apt to quarrel as thou art, any man should buy the fee-simple of my life for an hour and a quarter.

WILLIAM SHAKESPEARE *Romeo and Juliet*, Act III, scene 6

(*b*)

SIR OLIVER: Ha! Ha! ha! so my old friend is married, hey?—
a young wife out of the country.—Ha! ha! ha! that he should
have stood bluff to old bachelor so long, and sink into a
husband at last!

ROWLAND: But you must not rally him on the subject, Sir
Oliver; 'tis a tender point, I assure you, though he has been
married only seven months.

SIR OLIVER: Then he has been just half a year on the stool of
repentance!—Poor Peter!—But you say he has entirely given
up Charles—never sees him, hey?

ROWLAND: His prejudice against him is astonishing, and I am
sure greatly increased by a jealousy of him with Lady Teazle,
which he had been industriously led into by a scandalous
society in the neighbourhood, who have contributed not a
little to Charles's ill name. Whereas the truth is, I believe, if
the lady is partial to either of them, his brother is the favourite

SIR OLIVER: Aye, I know there are a set of malicious, prating,
prudent gossips, both male and female, who murder characters to kill time; and will rob a young fellow of his good name,
before he has years to know the value of it.—But I am not to
be prejudiced against my nephew by such, I promise you.—
No, no,—if Charles has done nothing false or mean, I shall
compound for his extravagance.

RICHARD BRINDSLEY SHERIDAN, *School for Scandal*,
Act II, Scene 3

(*c*)

PILOT OFFICER: I think you're a fool, Airman. God knows
why the Air Ministry send us fools. They never select, select
is the answer, select and pick those out from the others.

ANDREW: What others, sir?

PILOT OFFICER: Don't question me!

ANDREW: But I was only thinking of . . .

PILOT OFFICER: You aren't paid to think, Airman, don't you
know that? You aren't paid to think . . . No, it's no good
trying that line . . . Why pretend? I don't really frighten you,
do I? I don't really frighten you, but you obey my orders,

nevertheless. It's a funny thing. We have always ruled, but I suspect we've never frightened you. I know that as soon as I turn my back you'll merely give me a 'V' sign and make a joke of me to the others, won't you? And they'll laugh. Especially Thompson. He knows you're not frightened, that's why he's in the ranks. But I'll break him. Slumming, that's all he's doing, slumming. What's your name?

ARNOLD WESKER, *Chips with Everything*, Act I, Scene 5

It is clear that while all these passages are English, they are different sorts of English. In the first two passages the meaning may in general be understood by most present-day readers, but there will be some words or phrases about which there is likely to be doubt unless the reader has made a study of the language of the period. Equally parts of the third passage would create difficulties for Shakespeare or Sheridan were they to be here to read them. In the first passage, for instance, the meaning of 'thou wilt tutor me from quarrelling', or 'the fee-simple of my life' may be deduced from the context, but represent unfamiliar uses of familiar words; similarly in the second passage 'stood bluff to old bachelor' or 'I shall compound for his extravagance' may be unfamiliar expressions to most people. The third passage has expressions that may present difficulty even to older people still alive now: 'trying that line', or 'give me a "V" sign' —though the latter may present as much difficulty to the very young as to the very old. Even where meaning is not in doubt, however, the grammatical patterning of the first two passages is in some measure different from that of the third, and even though this may not impede understanding, it is often quite unlike anything in use today. The use of 'thou' with its verb forms 'art' or 'wilt quarrel', the use of 'an' and a subjunctive form where we might use 'if' and an indicative form; these and other features are all strange to a speaker of modern English. The structures in the second passage are on the whole much more familiar, but even here some would be unnatural in modern colloquial speech, such as 'a jealousy of him with Lady Teazle'.

The differences are of course, to be accounted for by the fact that the first passage was written roughly 200 years before the second, and the second roughly 200 years before the third. The surprising thing is that while many people are aware of the fact that the language of Shakespeare's time is not the same as that of Sheridan's, and that Wesker's language is obviously different from either, they are yet unwilling to face the implication that the English of today must be equally transient and that the English of 2168 will make the English of 1968 appear quaint and old fashioned. Some people take the attitude that language change is something that happened in the past, but must not be allowed to happen in the future. If new words are introduced, or old words are used in a different way; if 'good' writers use allegedly incorrect grammar; if public speakers use a form of pronunciation unfamiliar to certain other speakers; then there will be cries of the 'corruption' or 'deterioration' of the English language. Thus B.B.C. announcers have been reviled for using an / r / sound instead of a glottal stop in 'law and order', and there have recently been angry letters to *The Times* protesting against the collocation of 'sophisticated' and 'technology', coupled with appeals for the restoration of the 'true' meaning of 'sophisticated'. Resentment and righteous anger often accompany such attempts at stemming the tide.

It is however, necessary to recognise that, much as we may dislike the facts of language change as applied to our own version of English, such change is apparently inexorable. Even in the course of relatively few years, often within a generation, the commonly accepted pronunciation of a vowel, or a word may change. If you listen to older R.P. speakers saying 'go home' you may well find that they say / gou houm / while young people are far more likely to say something like / gəu həum /. Meanings and uses of words also change, and many entertaining books have been written tracing the changes of meaning in words over the centuries. Grammatical usage changes, even if more slowly. But again, what is entertaining in the past, is so often and so illogically seen as anathema in the present. No one now would seriously advocate returning to the use of 'sad' as meaning 'having had one's fill, sated,' but there are many who dislike the use of 'take it' in the modern sense of 'I can take it'

164

= 'I can endure with fortitude'. Equally, even although 'guts' in the sense of 'spirit, force of character' has been used since 1893, people are still found insisting that its only 'correct' meaning is the older one of 'the contents of the abdominal cavity'.

Resistance to any change in the forms and uses of the language which was acquired in childhood is common amongst many people, not only in England, but also in other countries, sometimes to the extent of official attempts being made to 'preserve the purity' of the language. At the same time, strangely enough, that branch of language study which has at any rate until recently, been most advanced in western countries is the historical study of language. **Historical linguistics** consists of the study of language changes, what has caused them, and what are the results of such changes on the language itself and on other associated languages. Another branch of linguistic study closely related to such historical studies is **comparative linguistics** (often called **comparative philology**), where comparisons are made between different languages. The previous chapter referred to contrastive linguistics, where two languages were compared in order to find areas of difference, usually with the specific aim of isolating teaching points, but comparative linguistics is a more wide-ranging and rather differently orientated study. Contrastive linguistics is a **synchronic** study, i.e. it deals with two languages as both are, or are arbitrarily assumed to be, at any given point of time. Comparative linguistics, in its most usual sense[1] is **diachronic**, i.e. it is concerned with relationships between languages over periods of time. Historical and comparative linguistic studies were carried to relatively advanced stages in the last century, largely as a result of the stimulus given to such studies by the discovery that Sanskrit, the ancient classical language of India, could be indisputably linked with the more familiar Latin, Greek and German languages.

---

1. A further area of study is that sometimes called 'typological comparison', which is essentially concerned with classification of the systems and structures of different languages irrespective of their language families, or their relationship to each other.

Any English speaker who has learnt German, to however elementary a stage, will have very soon become aware that many words in German are like English words. English 'foot', German 'Fuss', English 'hand' German 'Hand', English 'come' German 'kommen', English 'winter' German 'Winter', these and many other words are seen to be similar. Or if, with a knowledge of French, he turns to Italian or Spanish, he soon realises that many words in these three languages are alike:

English	*French*	*Italian*	*Spanish*
foot	pied	piede	pie
hand	main	mano	mano

It may not, however, have occurred to him to wonder why this should be so; or to find out what determines that English and German have forms in common, forms which are different from the common French, Italian and Spanish forms. Other word forms can be found which show a similarity through all five (and more) languages:

English	*German*	*French*	*Italian*	*Spanish*
two	zwei	deux	due	dos
mother	Mutter	mère	madre	madre
me	mich	moi	me	me

What is chiefly of interest is to realise, not only in these cases, but also even where similarities are not so apparent, that there are sometimes systematic correspondences, too frequent to be explained as mere coincidence. Italian 'piede' and English 'foot' may not appear very alike, but in many words an initial English / f / has a corresponding Italian / p /. Compare for instance English 'father', Italian 'padre', English 'fish', Italian 'pesce'. Or again, as between English and German, there are certain systematic correspondences between English 'd' and German 't': English 'drink', German 'trinken', English 'door', German 'Tur', English 'dream', German 'Traum'.

Linguists struck with such systematic correspondences, which exist over many languages, set out to search for and explain the reasons which lead to these facts. One obvious answer—that languages had 'borrowed' words from each other—could only be valid for relatively small numbers of words. It was unlikely, to say the least, that words in such common and universal use as 'hand', 'foot', 'two', etc., should all be borrowed words. The explanation seemed to lie in the fact that the slightly differing word forms all derived ultimately from some common source, but had, over the centuries, all gradually changed in their own peculiar and unique ways. This explanation corresponded with other known facts, and from this basis linguists (or philologists as they were called then), were able to build up pictures of the relationship the various languages had to each other. This is illustrated (necessarily in a formalised and over-simplified way) in the diagram and notes on the following page, which show the relationships of some of the languages in use today.

The reasons why such changes take place, so that eventually two languages become mutually incomprehensible, although they derive from the same source, are partly, though perhaps not wholly understood. One of the more obvious reasons is the geographical spread, and in earlier times subsequent isolation from each other, of people who originally had the same language. The best documented illustration of this is the development of Latin into the various Romance languages. Large areas of Europe were occupied for several centuries by the Romans, and in these areas spoken Latin became a status symbol and the official and widely used language, displacing for many purposes the local languages of those areas. Even when the Roman Empire collapsed and the barbarians arrived, there were enough speakers of Latin to ensure that its use continued. But as the cohesiveness of the Empire vanished, the Latin in each of these areas gradually changed, differently in each area, until speakers even in neighbouring areas became increasingly unintelligible to each other. With the constraints of the Empire removed, the need for mutual intelligibility was removed and contacts lessened, or even vanished.

The same process of change and diversification from a common source can be seen continuing today. The English with which most of us are familiar—Standard English—is now the language of only a small minority of the world's English speakers. The English language was taken by emigrants over

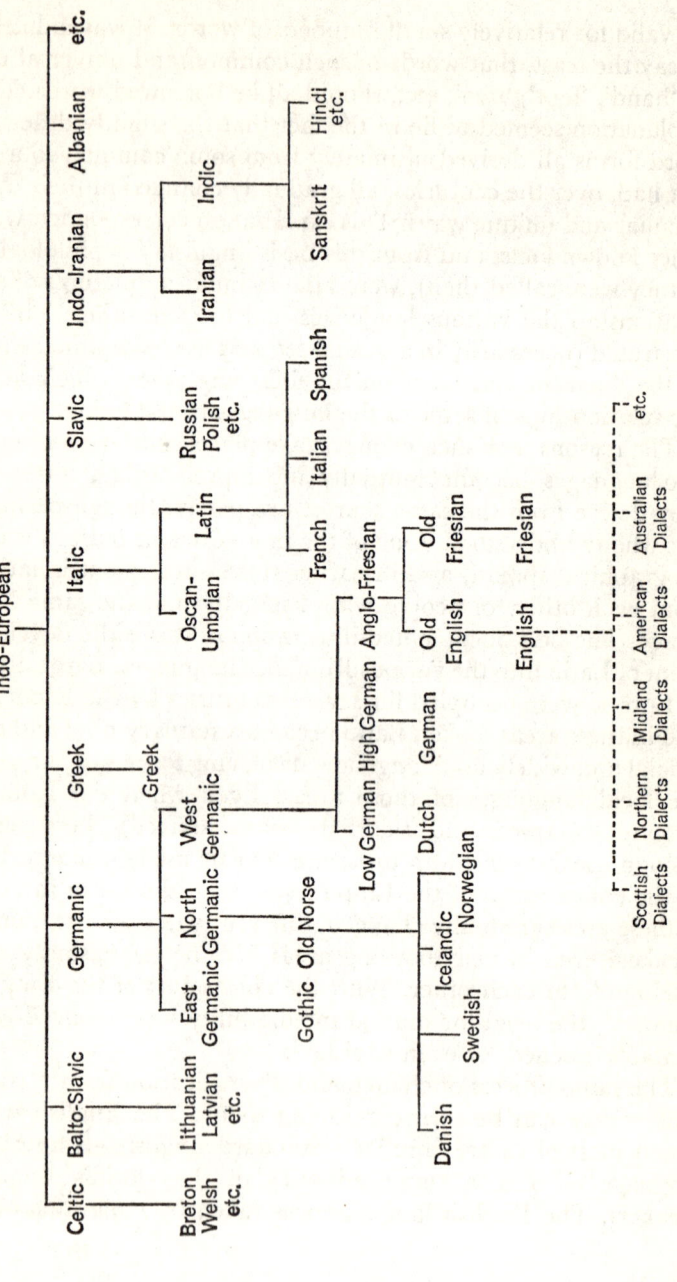

NOTES TO LANGUAGE 'TREE' DIAGRAM

1. The existence of a language 'Indo-European' is inferred, not known. No remnant of it exists anywhere, but evidence suggests that it must have existed, perhaps in forms something like those the linguists have been able to infer, on the basis of the sort of correspondences discussed in the text, but carried over many more languages. 'Indo-European' cannot be taken necessarily to represent any one language, but may itself represent a set of mutually comprehensible dialects from which the various language families such as Italic or Germanic ultimately derive.

2. The Indo-European language family covers most of Europe and Northern India, and has more recently spread to the Americas, Australasia and Asiatic Russia. But other language families exist even in Europe, e.g. the Finno-Ugrian family, which is represented by Finnish, Hungarian and Estonian. Outside Europe there are the Sino-Tibetan family (Chinese languages, Thai, etc.), the Hamito-Semitic family (Arabic, Hebrew, Maltese etc.), the Dravidian family (Central and southern Indian languages, Malay, Malagasy, etc.), numerous African language families, North American Indian language families, and others.

3. It should be realised that many stages can coexist. Language change and development is comparatively slow, and there will be long periods when older forms coexist with emerging forms. There is no fixed or ascertainable point at which Latin becomes French, or Italian. This will be realised if the subdivisions of English at the foot of the tree are seen. Any of these English dialects may die out, or may replace 'English', or may itself subdivide or develop into some other language form.

4. Some parts of the tree are shown in more detail than others, i.e. more intervening stages between Indo–European and the modern languages are shown.

---

to the American continent several centuries ago, as it was also to South Africa. It was exported to Australia and New Zealand, and is also widely used in Africa, the Indian subcontinent and in other parts of the Far East. In all these places it is still recognisably English that is spoken, but in each area the language has its own distinctive forms. The differences lie partly in vocabulary and grammar, but more perhaps in the sound of the language—vowels particularly, vary widely in each of these areas. Yet historically we know that all derive ultimately from the English spoken in this country. The processes of change are in all probability slowed up by the fact that contacts between these regions are now much more frequent than was possible before the invention of radio and television, or the more wide-spread circulation of the written forms of the language such as newspapers and books, and the frequent personal intercourse between people from the different areas. There is also a conscious desire on the part of many English speakers to prevent the breakdown of mutual intelligibility, so that it is perhaps unlikely that the process will be carried as far as it was with Latin.

Other factors than geography however, must be called in to explain some of the changes. The three samples of English quoted at the beginning of this chapter were all written in almost identical geographical locations, and yet show great changes. The internal changes in a language, which are independent of geography or other external pressures, are manifest in all languages but the reasons for them have not yet been satisfactorily explained. As speech is transmitted from one generation to another, variations are gradually introduced in pronunciation, grammar and use of words, and eventually become widespread, or universal to all speakers of the language. Even with such apparently arbitrary changes however, there is often a surprising degree of systematisation, so that, for instance, in one area there may be a wholesale shift in the pronunciation of plosive consonants; all plosives may change from being unaspirated to being aspirated, or aspirated plosives may become fricatives. The London dialectal pronunciation of aspirated plosives i.e. / tʰi: / (tea) often approaches that of a fricative / tˢi: /, and this might well become more common over the years.

Yet another reason for change may lie in external pressures other than that of geographical diversity. Sometimes the speakers of a language are strongly influenced by the overlay of another language, as when a country is occupied or dominated by a foreign power. In these circumstances people may continue to use their native language, but it will be affected by the language of the dominating power. Such influence may consist largely of speakers borrowing words from the other language.

English, as the tree diagram shows, is basically a Germanic language, but has very many Romance type words, derived largely from a process of borrowing during various periods of 'Romance' domination, such as the Roman conquest or the Norman conquest. Modern Welsh shows many signs of English influence, and the speakers of many African languages have incorporated words taken from the languages of the colonial powers. Words are often borrowed from the foreign language, but are given the morphological and phonological characteristics of the indigenous language, so that sometimes they almost lose their original identity. A newcomer to Africa may take some time to realise the origin of / səkəru:dəreibə / 'sukurudereibe' in 'screwdriver', or / baiskəli: / 'baiskeli' in 'bicycle'. There have been complaints in recent years about the importation of English words into Japanese, where they are given the syllabic values of Japanese, and so Japanese women go to the hairdresser for a 'pama' or 'shyanpu-setto', returning home afterwards by a 'takushi' or a 'basu'.

The influences of another language may be reflected other than in the borrowing and reshaping of words. Sometimes a new language form will result, as with so-called **pidgin** languages. Pidgin may be described as 'a language with very drastically reduced structure and vocabulary and native to none of its users'.[1] There are many examples known of pidgin throughout the world, some of which have vanished, others of which have developed into **creoles** (see below). Well known examples of pidgin have been the original pidgin used for trading purposes between Chinese and British, but now almost disappeared, the American Indian pidgin English, which survives only artificially and inaccurately in children's comics in such alleged utterances as 'me heap big chief', Melanesian pidgin used throughout New Guinea, and two pidgins which are now largely creolised—West African pidgin, one of whose 'descendants' is Krio, the language of Freetown, Sierra Leone, and Jamaican Creole, originally a Caribbean pidgin. What is sometimes called 'Kitchen Swahili' or 'Ki-Settler' is another

1. Robert A. Hall Jnr., 'How Pidgin English has evolved', *New Scientist*, 16th February, 1961.

example, where European housewives speaking to African servants in East Africa frequently used a language which was not recognisably English or Swahili, but consisted often of Anglicised Swahili, or Swahili-ised English vocabulary grafted on to either English or Swahili grammatical patterning. A cookery book published by a European women's organisation in Kenya (first published in 1928 but frequently republished up until the 1950s) included a language section headed 'Orders to Servants' and gave the English, Kiswahili and Ki-Settler translations:

English	Kiswahili	Ki-Settler
Dust well, do not flick with the duster.	Panguse na kitambaa, usipige.	Piga dusta.
Clean the knives.	Safishe visu.	Polishi kisu.
Make toast.	Chome mkate.	Choma toasti.

Pidgin may disappear if social conditions render it unnecessary or undesirable, or it may develop into a creole—'a language which has grown out of a pidgin by its becoming the native tongue of a speech community'. The 'West Indian English' in its more extreme forms, which can give teachers and children so much trouble when West Indian immigrants send their children to school in this country, is in fact a creole—a language in process of development. It has its own valid phonology, structure and vocabulary, much of which can be derived from seventeenth century English, but which also show West African language influence.

This is perhaps the point at which to try to dispel the myths of 'primitive' languages. It is sometimes thought that the languages spoken by peoples who are less technologically or scientifically advanced must be 'primitive' in the sense that they are crude, fragmentary or inadequate; it is sometimes even thought that they have 'no grammar' or are linguistically undeveloped. Such naïve ideas do not bear investigation. Such languages have in fact very highly developed and complex structural patterns and are capable of great subtlety of expression in those areas where subtlety is required. They may, of course, lack vocabulary for things which are not a part of their culture, but this is true of any language, however 'advanced' its speakers may be technologically. All languages are required by their speakers to grow with, or adapt to, the social and cultural environment, and no language is inherently incapable of doing so. Whatever its speakers want it to do, or need it to do, a language can do. Robert A. Hall, in the article referred to above, quoted the Florentine G. B. Belli, who, over four centuries ago, said in connection with the rise of Italian 'all languages are suitable for expressing the thoughts and needs of those who use them; and if they are not so, those who use them make them so.'

If anyone doubts this, perhaps the following examples of mid-twentieth century English will be sufficient to convince him that English too is changing, adapting to 'the thoughts and needs' of its users. What one thinks of the 'thoughts and needs' is, of course, not a language matter.

1. The insulation of the external instrument as a cause of the type of social change illustrated by our third group appears to rest on unwarranted assumptions, on assumptions of the kind we have found to be back of one-way deterministic theories. In the first place the indifferent instrument cannot be held responsible for the uses to which it is put. In the second place, since the instrument is indifferent, it can be made to speak with many voices, supplying to the different groups the different appeals that are severally congenial to hem.

R. M. MacIver, *Social Causation*
Harper & Row

2. *For faster programming*

    WATCH
    YOUR
    LANGUAGE

Now I.C.T. offer a commercial language compiler that gets a computer into action quicker—and so makes it productive earlier. New 1900 Series COBOL is a full-scale COBOL. Written in basic English in a standard format, it is easy to learn, write and amend. And it can be used on computers costing as little as £70,000.

Savings from the outset
The new full-scale COBOL compiler has programs ready, tested and running much quicker because it needs only one-fifth of the program-writing time of low-level languages and one-fifth the (assembly code) debugging time.

(Advertisement)

3. Considering first the three-covalent nitrogen atom, the two most likely shapes for the valency disposition are plane triangular or pyramidal. The fact that, as yet, no compounds of the formula Nyxz have been resolved into the enantiomorphs theoretically possible for the pyramidal form, is a good example of how dangerous negative evidence can be. It is, in fact, known that in addition to the three covalent electron pairs nitrogen has to accommodate a lone pair of non-bonding electrons and that these four pairs are to be found at the corners of a distorted tetrahedron. The substituent groups thus form a pyramid with the nitrogen atom and the two enantiomorphic forms must be too easily interconverted and therefore rapidly racemised, for resolution to be possible. Fairly recent compounds have been resolved in which the three covalencies are fixed into their positions by incorporation into a condensed ring system so that they are no longer able to 'umbrella' inside out.

D. E. P. Hughes and M. J. Maloney *Advanced Theoretical Chemistry*
Chatto & Windus

4. *I saw the best minds of my generation destroyed by madness,*
    starving hysterical naked,
    dragging themselves through the Negro streets at dawn looking for
    an angry fix
    angelheaded hipsters burning for the ancient heavenly connection to
    the starry dynamo in the machinery of night,
    who poverty and tatters and hollow-eyed and high sat up smoking

in the supernatural darkness of cold-water flats floating across
    the tops of cities contemplating jazz,
who bared their brains to heaven under the El and saw Mohamedan
    angels staggering on tenement roofs illuminated,

etc.

Allen Ginsberg, *Howl*

5. These bright elects, consentconsorted, they were waltzing up their willside with their princesome handsome angeline chiuff while in those wherebus there wont bears way (meaning unknown, a place where pigeons carry fire to seethe viands, a miry hill, belge and sore footh) oaths and screams and bawley groans with a belchybubhub and a hellabelow bedemmed and bediabbled the araimining lucisphere.

James Joyce, *Finnegans Wake*, Faber

6. *Gold of kingcups*
    coaxed blossoming of an
    album-destined smile
    click of camera
    tick of indicator and turn for home
    burst of open-roaded open-engine song
    spacious smooth as Wilton carpet ride
    moments of your
    family sports car years—
    your best-of-both-worlds
    driving years.
    MG 1300—sports car performance
    family style
    at MG dealers.

(Advertisement)

Suggestions for Further Reading

Abercrombie, David. *Studies in Phonetics and Linguistics*. O.U.P. 1965.
This is a collection of papers written over a long space of time. Some are more relevant than others to the student beginning a study of linguistics. Of particular interest are the first two, on 'Conversation and Spoken Prose', and on 'R.P. and Local Accent'.

Billows, F. L. *The Techniques of Language Teaching*. Longmans. 1961.
Very useful for anyone proposing to teach a foreign language—especially English as a foreign language, but also of very considerable interest to anyone wishing to follow up some of the ideas outlined in the present volume.

Firth, J. R. *The Tongues of Men* and *Speech*. O.U.P. 1964.
These two short works were originally published in 1937 and 1930 respectively but have only relatively recently been reprinted. They are the most easily readable of Firth's writing, and are of value in showing the origins of much of British thinking on linguistics. *The Tongues of Men* in particular, is of relevance still.

Flower, F. D. *Language and Education*. Longmans 1966.
The author points out that 'the most important subject not yet taught in teacher training is English language . . .' and devotes much of the book to showing the importance of considering language in all aspects of education.

Gimson, A. C. *An Introduction to the Pronunciation of English*. Edward Arnold 1962.
A full and useful introduction to the study of phonetics and phonology. It includes detailed descriptions of the sounds of English, including notes on historical changes, and advice to foreign learners on articulation.

Gleason, H. A. *An Introduction to Descriptive Linguistics*. Holt, Rinehart & Winston. 1961 (Revised Edition)
Designed for use as a textbook in America, this is a clear and useful introduction to the study of language, which uses many different languages for illustration of methods and techniques of language analysis. There is an accompanying workbook. It does, of course concentrate almost exclusively on American work in the field, and terminology is American.

176

Halliday, M. A. K., McIntosh, Angus and Strevens, Peter. *The Linguistic Sciences and Language Teaching*. Longmans. 1964.
This contains one of the few relatively accessible accounts of scale and category theory. Some parts of the book are easier to read than others, but anyone seriously interested in linguistics in England will find it essential reading.

Lawton, Denis. *Social Class, Language and Education*. Routledge and Kegan Paul. 1968.
This includes a critique of the work of Bernstein on language and social class, and also accounts of the author's own research on children and certain aspects of their language. Readable and useful on the sociolinguistics side.

McIntosh, Angus, & Halliday, M.A.K. *Patterns of Language: Papers in genaral, descriptive and applied linguistics*. Longmans. 1966.
A most interesting collection of papers on a varied selection of topics, ranging from several papers on the application of linguistics to literary studies, to one on linguistics and machine translation. The unifying theme is the demonstration of linguistic patterning.

O'Connor, D. J. and Arnold, G. F. *The Intonation of Colloquial English. A Practical Handbook*. Longmans. 1961.
As the subtitle indicates, intensely practical. Although designed primarily to help foreign learners of English, it is of great value in showing the native speaker some of the complexities which he masters without effort.

Quirk, R. *The Use of English*. Longmans. 1962.
Very readable and entertaining, designed to 'stimulate a mature and informed approach to our language', and based on very deep scholarship. It requires no prior knowledge of linguistics for an appreciative reading.

Rivers, Wilga. *The Psychologist and the Foreign Language Teacher*. University of Chicago Press. 1964.
An appraisal of modern methods of foreign language teaching in the light of learning theory as propounded by the various schools of psychology. It is designed primarily for the teacher of foreign languages, but has more general interest.

Sapir, E. *Language*. Harcourt Brace & World. 1921. Harvest Books reprint.
One of the 'foundation' books of modern linguistics, and one which appears almost automatically on every linguistics reading list ever compiled, and with justice. First published in 1921, it is still very relevant.

Strevens, Peter. *Papers in Language and Language Teaching*. O.U.P. 1965.
A collection of papers on topics covering a wide range, from phonetics to the problems of teaching English in Africa. Mainly of interest to language teachers, but some papers of more general interest.

Suggestions for Further Reading

Sturtevant, E. H. *An Introduction to Linguistic Science*. Yale University Press (Paperback) 1960.

A clear and readable account of some areas not always covered in elementary books, such as phonetic 'laws' and the origins and development of language.

Thomas, Owen. *Transformational Grammar and the Teacher of English*. Holt, Rinehart & Winston. 1965.

One of the very few easily readable accounts of transformational grammar for the beginner. It claims to be a 'pedagogical rather than a scientific grammar' and its emphasis is on practical and teaching matters, but nevertheless it provides a very useful way in for anyone interested in TG.

Selected Bibliography

The following are amongst the books and periodicals which have been most useful in compiling the present volume. The list cannot be fully comprehensive.

Abercrombie, David, *Studies in Phonetics and Linguistics*. London. O.U.P., 1965.

Abercrombie, David, *Elements of General Phonetics*. Edinburgh. Edinburgh University Press, 1967.

Austin, J. L., *How to do things with Words*. (Ed. J. O. Urmson.) Oxford University Press, 1962.

Bazell, C. E., and others (Ed.) *In Memory of J. R. Firth*. London. Longmans, 1966.

Bennett, W. A. J., *Aspects of Language and Language Teaching*. Cambridge. Cambridge University Press, 1968.

Bernstein, Basil, *A Socio-linguistic Approach to Social Learning*. (In Penguin Survey of the Social Sciences, 1965). Penguin Books, 1965.

Billows, F. L., *The Techniques of Language Teaching*. London. Longmans, 1961.

Bloomfield, L., *Language*. New York. Holt, 1933.

Carroll, J. B., *The Study of Language*. Cambridge, Mass. Harvard U.P. (London: O.U.P.), 1953.

Chomsky, N., *Syntactic Structures*. The Hague: Mouton (Janua Linguarum 4), 1957.

Chomsky, N., *Aspects of the Theory of Syntax*. Cambridge, Mass. M.I.T. Press, 1965.

Chomsky, N., A Review of B. F. Skinner's 'Verbal Behaviour'. (In *Language*, 35, No. 1 (1959). Reprinted in *The Structure of Language*, ed. Fodor and Katz. Prentice-Hall Inc., 1964.

Chomsky, N., *Cartesian Linguistics*. Harper and Row. 1966.

Crystal, David and Quirk, Randolph. *Systems of Prosodic and Paralinguistic Features in English*. The Hague: Mouton & Co. (Janua Linguarum. 39) 1964.

Crystal, David, *What is Linguistics?* London: Edward Arnold, 2nd edn. 1969.

Diringer, David, *The Alphabet*. London. Hutchinson, 1949.

Enkvist, Nils Erik, Spencer, John and Gregory, Michael J., *Linguistics and Style*. London O.U.P. 1964.

Firth, J. R., *Papers in Linguistics. 1934–1951*. London. O.U.P., 1957.

Firth, J. R., *The Tongues of Men* and *Speech*. London. O.U.P., 1964.

Bibliography

Flower, F. D., *Language and Education*. London. Longmans, 1966.

Fries, C. C. *The Structure of English*. New York. Harcourt Brace 1952; London: Longmans 1957.

Gimson, A. C., *An Introduction to the Pronunciation of English*. London. Edward Arnold, 1962.

Gleason, H. A. *An Introduction to Descriptive Linguistics*. Revised Edit. Holt, Rinehart & Winston, 1961.

Gleason, H. A., *Linguistics and English Grammar*. Holt, Rinehart & Winston, 1965.

Gregory, Michael J., Enkvist, Nils Erik and Spencer, John. See under Enkvist.

Halliday, M. A. K., *Categories of the Theory of Grammer*. (In Word **17**. Journal of the Linguistic Circle of New York.)

Halliday, M. A. K., McIntosh, Angus, and Strevens, Peter. *The Linguistic Sciences and Language Teaching*. London. Longmans, 1964.

Hayakawa, S. I., *Language in Thought and Action*. New York. Harcourt Brace, 1949: London. George Allen & Unwin, 1952.

Hill, A. A., *Introduction to Linguistic Structures*. New York. Harcourt Brace, 1958.

Hockett, Charles F. *A Course in Modern Linguistics*. New York. Macmillan, 1958.

Hornby, A. S., *A Guide to Patterns and Usage in English*. London. O.U.P., 1954.

Jones, Daniel. *The Pronunciation of English*. Fourth Edition. Cambridge. University Press, 1966.

Kufner, Herbert L., *The Grammatical Structures of English and German*. Chicago. University of Chicago Press, 1962.

Lado, Robert, *Language Teaching*. Boston. McGraw-Hill, 1964.

Lado, Robert, *Linguistics Across Cultures*. Ann Arbor: Michigan U.P., 1957.

Lenneberg, E. H. (ed.), *New Directions in the study of Language*. M.I.T. Press, 1964.

Mackey, W. F., *Language Teaching Analysis*. London. Longmans, 1965.

Malinowski, B., *Coral Gardens and Their Magic*. Allen and Unwin, 1965. (New York, 1935).

Miller, George, *Language and Communication*. New York. McGraw-Hill, 1951.

Miller, George (see Smith, Frank and Miller, George).

Ogden, C. K. and Richards, I. A., *The Meaning of Meaning*. London. Routledge & Kegan Paul. Tenth Edit., 1949.

O'Connor, D. J., and Arnold, G. F., *Intonation of Colloquial English*. London. Longmans, 1961.

Palmer, F. R., *A Linguistic Study of the English Verb*. London. Longmans, 1965.

Palmer, H. E., *The Oral Method of Teaching Languages*. Cambridge. Heffer, 1923.

Palmer, H. E., *Principles of Language Study*. New York. World Book Co., 1921. London. O.U.P., 1964.

Palmer, H. E., *Specimens of English Construction Patterns*. Tokyo. Dept. of Education, 1934.

Piaget, Jean, *The Language and Thought of the Child*. Tr. Marjorie and Ruth Gabain. London. Routledge & Kegan Paul, 1960.

Plowden Report, *Children and Their Primary Schools*. H.M.S.O., 1967.

Quirk, R., *The Use of English*. London. Longmans, 2nd edn. 1964.

Quirk, R. and Crystal, David, see under Crystal.

Rivers, Wilga, *The Psychologist and the Foreign Language Teacher*. Chicago. University of Chicago Press, 1964.

Rivers, Wilga, *Teaching Foreign Language Skills*. Chicago and London. University of Chicago Press, 1968.

Roberts, Paul, *English Sentences*. New York. Harcourt Brace, 1962.

Robins, R. H., *General Linguistics: An Introductory Survey*. London. Longmans, 1964.

Rosenberg, S. (ed.), *Directions in Psycholinguistics*. New York. Macmillan, 1965.

Sapir, E., *Language*. New York, Harcourt Brace, 1921, Reprint Harvest Books 1949.

de Saussure, F., *Cours de Linguistique Générale*. Paris, Payot, 1965.

Smith, Frank and Miller, George. (ed.), *The Genesis of Language*. Cambridge, Mass. M.I.T., 1966.

Spencer, J., Gregory, M. J. and Enkvist, N. E. See under Enkvist.

Strang, B. M. H., *Modern English Structure*. London. Edward Arnold, 2nd edn. 1968.

Strevens, P. D., *Papers in Language and Language Teaching*. London. O.U.P., 1965.

Sturtevant, E. H., *An Introduction to Linguistic Science*. New Haven, Yale University Press, 1947; Yale Paperback, 1960.

Thomas, Owen, *Transformational Grammar and the Teacher of English*. New York. Holt, Rinehart and Winston, 1965.

Vygotsky, L. S., *Thought and Language*. Cambridge, Mass. M.I.T., 1966.

Whorf, B. L., *Language, Thought and Reality*. New York. Wiley, 1956.

Wilkinson, Andrew, and others, *Spoken English*. University of Birmingham. Education Review. Occasional Publications Number Two, 1965.

PERIODICALS

English Language Teaching. O.U.P. in association with British Council.

Language Learning. Ann Arbor: Michigan.

Journal of Linguistics. Cambridge University Press for Linguistics Association of Great Britain.

Index

Index

historical linguistics, 165
intonation, 16, 46–54, 59, 129, 135, 136, 150
levels of language, 13, 130–1, 136
lexis, *see vocabulary*
lexical item, 74
    words, 68, 69, 131, 139, 153
literature, 8–9, 15, 17–19, 90, 91, 94, 142, 146, 147–8
Luria, A. R., 111
meaning, 4–5, 6, 48, 51, 59, 60, 64, 69–70, 112, 117, 122, 127, 131–2, 135, 136, 147, 153, 163, 164
    word, 86–98, 158
modes of discourse, 16, 108–10
morpheme, 62–6, 68, 92, 104, 135
names, 5, 87–8, 134
noun, 55, 60–1, 69–70, 71, 125, 126
oral method, 149, 154
paralinguistic features, 49–50
performance, 123, 149
phatic communion, 3, 4, 6, 7, 12
phoneme, phonemics, 23–5, 29–30, 37–45, 46–58, 136, 137, 138
phonology, 23–5, 131, 136
phonetics, 23–5, 26–9, 30–7, 46–58, 103, 131, 155
Piaget, J., 111, 119
pidgin, 171–2
Plowden Report, 141
psychology and psychologists, 9, 11, 12, 86, 95, 111, 114, 117, 118, 119, 127–8, 138–9, 148–9
psycholinguistics, 119, 128
Received Pronunciation (RP), 24, 104–5, 164
register, 105, 107–10, 145, 146, 152, 159
root, 64
de Saussure, F. 116–17, 123
scale and category grammar, *see grammar*
semantic(s), 131, 135, 155, 157
    field, 96–8, 157
    see also meaning
sentence, 50, 62, 77–85, 150–1, 156
situational method, 149, 151–4
Skinner, B. F., 148–9

social class, language and, 24, 99–106
society, language and, 3, 4, 12, 14–15, 91, 95, 97, 111–13, 116, 117–19, 127, 129, 136, 147, 171–3
sociolinguistics, 119
spoken language, 14–22, 67–8, 82 108, 142, 147, 150
    see also phonetics and children
standard English, *see English*
stress, 16, 47–8, 54–8
structure, 59–85 pass., 90, *see also grammar*
structural linguistics, 122–3
    method, 149–51, 154
style, 94, 109–10
substance, 122, 131
symbols, 21, 22
    phonetic, 27–8
symbolic nature of language, 132–5, 143
synchronic study, 165
syntax, 139, 141, *see also grammar*
systems, language, 12–13, 129, 132, 135, 136
tenor of discourse, 109
thought, language and 9–10, 12, 139, 146
transformational–generative grammar (TG), *see grammar*
translation, 10, 98, 149, 150, 153
verb, 60, 69, 70, 73–5, 77, 82, 125 126
vocabulary (lexis), 100, 109, 112, 113, 131, 139, 140, 152, 155, 169, 171, 172
    see also words
vowel, 26, 56, 103, 106, 129, 136, 155, 164
    cardinal vowel system, 35–7, 155
    English vowels, 37–9, 44–5
Vygotsky, L., 111, 119, 138
words, 47–8, 56–7, 59, 62, 66–9, 86–98, 103, 129, 132, 139, 157, 163, 166–7, 171
written language, 14–22, 131, 147, 150, 154

184